HARROW PAST

Acknowledgements

No local historian can hope to write a history, however incomplete, of a specific place without the help of archivists, librarians and other historians who have previously worked on the area: in this instance, T.L. Bartlett, Patricia Clarke, Elizabeth Cooper, Win Cunnington, Ron Edwards, Arthur Dark, Walter W. Druett, Jim Golland, Geoffrey Hewlett and H.M. Wilkins. I should particularly like to acknowledge the assistance given me by Bob Thompson of Harrow Civic Centre Library in finding general information, but especially for undertaking the onerous task of reading and correcting the text. (Any errors left are entirely my own.) He also made available from the archives most of the prints and photographs which have been reproduced.

I should like to thank Geoffrey Hewlett of Wembley for permission to use previously published pictures of that area and the *Harrow Observer* for allowing the use of some of their photographs.

The Illustrations

We are grateful to the following for permission to reproduce illustrations:
Eileen M. Bowlt: *1, 3, 4, 7, 8, 37, 62, 70, 87, 97, 113, 163, 165, 182*
The London Borough of Harrow: *jacket, frontispiece, 2, 6, 12, 13, 14, 15, 16, 17, 18, 19, 20, 21, 22, 23, 24, 25, 26, 28, 30, 31, 32, 33, 34, 35, 36, 38, 40, 41, 42, 43, 44, 46, 47, 48, 49, 50, 51, 52, 52, 54, 55, 56, 57, 58, 59, 60, 65, 66, 67, 71, 72, 73, 74, 75, 76, 77, 78, 79, 80, 81, 82, 83, 84, 86, 88, 90, 91, 92, 93, 96, 98, 99, 100, 101, 102, 103, 105, 109, 110, 111, 112, 114, 116, 117, 118, 119, 120, 122, 123, 124, 125, 126, 127, 128, 129, 130, 131, 132, 133, 134, 137, 138, 139, 140, 141, 142, 144, 145, 146, 148, 149, 150, 151, 152, 153, 154, 155, 157, 158, 159, 160, 166, 173, 174, 175, 176, 177, 178, 179, 181, 183, 184*
The Harrow Observer: *85, 147, 156*
Geoffrey Hewlett: *11, 27, 45, 164, 167, 168, 169, 170*
Historical Publications: *9, 64, 108, 115, 135*
London Metropolitan Archives: *5, 29, 63, 69, 89, 94, 95, 104, 106, 121, 143, 161, 162, 171, 172, 180*
London Transport Executive: *136*
National Monuments Record: *61*

First published 2000 by Historical Publications Ltd
32 Ellington Street, London N7 8PL (Tel: 020 -7607 1628)

ISBN 0 948667 65 6
British Library Cataloguing-in-Publication Data
A catalogue record for this book is available from the British Library

Typeset in Palatino by Historical Publications Ltd
Reproduction by G & J Graphics, London EC2
Printed in Zaragoza, Spain by Edelvives

HARROW PAST

Eileen M. Bowlt

HISTORICAL PUBLICATIONS

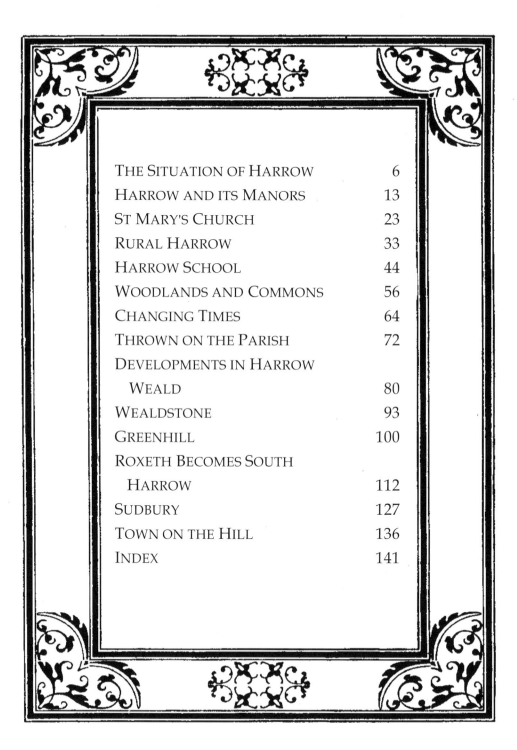

'View from Harrow Churchyard' looking out across Middlesex. Drawing by W. Luker jr, published in 1893.

1. Section of Rocque's map of Middlesex 1750, showing Grim's Dyke in the north to Sudbury in the south. The north-south main road to the right is today's Edgware Road.

The Situation of Harrow

Harrow in the year 2000 is probably regarded chiefly as a town with excellent shopping centres and easy connections with central London via the Metropolitan, Bakerloo Lines and National Railway, and notably as the home of a famous public school. Until relatively recently the Wealdstone part of Harrow in particular was quite industrial, with all kinds of factories producing anything from mattresses to brushes, but that era which started in the 1880s is now over.

To go back in history, Harrow was already a parish with its church perched on top of the hill before the Norman Conquest and by the time the Domesday Book was written in 1086 it was known as a manor. The bounds of medieval Harrow stretched far beyond the hill, encompassing Kenton, Preston, Uxendon, Wembley, Tokyngton, Alperton, Sudbury, Roxeth, Pinner, Greenhill (possibly first called Norbury) and the Weald. Its northern boundary was the shire ditch separating Middlesex from Hertfordshire and the eastern part of the irregular southern boundary was marked by the River Brent. The parishes of Ruislip, Northolt and Greenford adjoined Harrow on the west and south west and Great Stanmore and Kingsbury lay to the east.

Local government changes in 1894 and 1934 broke up this old pattern and in 1965 the London Borough of Harrow came into being, covering the medieval hamlets listed above, except for Wembley, Alperton and Tokyngton, and with the addition of Great and Little Stanmore. The latest population figure is 211,300.

This book will concentrate on the development of the central portion of the ancient parish, Harrow-on-the-Hill (or Harrow Town), Sudbury, Roxeth, Greenhill and Harrow Weald (the southern part of which developed into Wealdstone in the nineteenth century).

THE LIE OF THE LAND

The area is largely flat with Harrow Hill sticking up in the middle of the area and the land to the north of the hill rising gently through Wealdstone to the Uxbridge Road and thence more steeply to the county boundary. Southwards the land undulates towards the River Brent. Much of the

2. *A wintry view of Harrow-on-the-Hill by Allan Barraud, produced for the Pictorial World 24 January 1884.*

land in the south is little more than 100 feet above sea level, but Harrow Hill is more than 300 feet high and Harrow Weald rises above 400 feet (see Relief map opposite).

Most of the topsoil is heavy London Clay but the hill is composed of Claygate and Bagshot Beds which once covered all the London Clay. These beds have been eroded elsewhere, except at the top of Harrow Weald, where the Claygate Beds are exposed and have been partially covered by pebbly gravel drift deposits. These gravels are also to be found in the north west corner of Pinner. The only other geological beds to reach the surface in the Harrow area are the Reading Beds in Pinner, including Reading Sands at Waxwell (see Geological map opposite).

The lie of the land and the soils affected the settlement pattern of Harrow, with most of the inhabited areas being on land above 200 feet above sea level (see Relief map). Practically all the farmland, whether common fields or enclosed by the lord of the manor, was on the London Clay. The steeper land north of the Uxbridge Road was heavily wooded in earlier times and less readily cleared for ploughing. Most of the woodland is situated there to this day.

ROADS

Harrow was one of two places in north-west Middlesex, the other being Uxbridge, where main roads converged. Harrow had no national route like the London-Oxford-South Wales road through Uxbridge, but did have old routes, sometimes called shireways, linking it with other market towns and London. One from Watford and Bushey, through Harrow Weald, and Harrow Town continued south via Greenford and Osterley to Brentford and the Thames. Another from Rickmansworth through Pinner and Harrow Town became the Harrow Road to London. A third north-south route started at the Uxbridge Road and wound its way through Kenton to join the Harrow Road south of Wembley. The two major cross routes, the Uxbridge Road from Ruislip, through Hatch End and Harrow Weald; and the road from Roxeth, through Harrow and

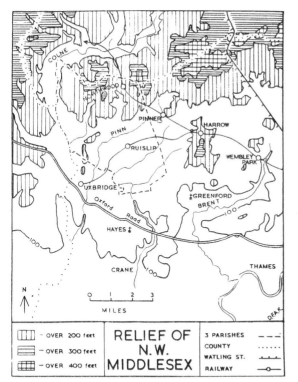

3. Relief map of north-west Middlesex (after D. F. A. Kiddle). Harrow Hill stands up from the surrounding plain.

Kenton, both joined the Edgware Road, a major road to London or the north. Numerous smaller lanes and tracks led into fields and surrounded the hamlets.

EARLIEST HARROW

Traces of early man in Middlesex have been found mainly along the valleys of the Thames, the Lea and the Colne. There is, so far, little evidence of prehistoric settlement in Harrow. The blade of a socketed axe was found at Harrow Weald c.1981;[1] a palstave was recorded at Pinner[2] and a barbed and tanged arrow head was dug out of a garden at Blythwood Road, Pinner in 1997.[3] Otherwise only a thin scattering of worked flints have been recorded, mainly across the high wooded land of Harrow Weald.

The purpose of the great earthwork known as Grim's Dyke, running through Harrow Weald, has not yet been determined. The latest archaeological excavation near the Grim's Dyke Hotel in 1979 found a hearth within the bank, probably used by workers at the period of construction, which has a radio carbon date of AD50, plus or minus 80 years.[4] This suggests that the earthwork dates from the first century AD, far too early to have been associated with Offa, king of Mercia. Earlier historians have suggested that the ditch and earthwork marked the southern boundary of his kingdom. Its position makes it unlikely to have been defensive, so it may have been a tribal boundary, built at the time of the Roman conquest of Britain after AD43. The Saxons who later settled the area probably named it Grim's Ditch, Grim meaning devil and the whole structure seeming to them to be the work of devils or giants.

A Roman pottery on Brockley Hill (Watling Street) in Stanmore produced large quantities of domestic ware between AD50 and 160 and excavations have produced evidence of occupation into the fourth century.[5] Three hoards of Roman coins have been found in Harrow, at Pinner Road, Priory Drive and Harrow Weald. Some cinerary urns and a Roman lamp have also turned up in a brick field.[6]

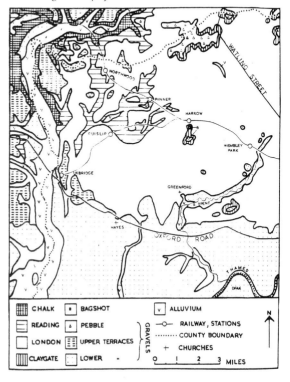

4. Geological map of north-west Middlesex.

5. *The tollgate cottage in London Road where the tollgate keeper lived. The tollgate itself was further down past the junction with Roxeth Hill.*

SAXON TIMES

The documented history of Harrow begins in 767 when Offa, king of Mercia exchanged 30 hides of land between 'Gumeninga Hergae' and the Lydding Brook and six hides and a dwelling house on the east side of the Lidding, with Abbot Stidberht for land in the Chilterns.[7] It is generally accepted by place name experts that *hearge* is an Old English word meaning a heathen holy place and that the Gumeningas were the followers of a man called Guma. The Lidding Brook runs into the Brent and higher tributaries like the Wealdstone Brook could have been called the Lidding in Saxon times. There has been much discussion about the exact locality of the 36 hides (one hide is reckoned at 120 acres) mentioned in Offa's charter. It is assumed that the Gumeningas' temple was on top of Harrow Hill and predated the spread of christianity among the Saxons. St Paul's in London had been established by 605, but the faith was adopted

patchily and the Gumeningas may have been around Harrow in the late seventh or early eighth centuries, unfortunately leaving no archaeological remains behind. It may well be with the Gumeningas that the continuous settlement of Harrow began. Pat Clarke has argued that the 30 hides granted to Stidberht could fit into the area between the Hill and the brook, that is Kenton, Alperton, part of Sudbury and central Harrow and that the six hides with a house sufficiently important to be mentioned is now Preston Road.[8] If one considers that Abbot Stidberht may have been the man who converted the pagan temple on the hill into a christian church, the house in the six hides may well have formed the priest's estate, hence the later name, Preston.

Later Saxon charters show that the 36 hides were still one estate when Cenulf of Mercia in 801 granted the lands to his companion, Pilheard

6. Grim's Dyke near Old Redding.

(probably only a grant for life). By 825, Cenulf's daughter, Cwoenthryth, Abbess of Southminster, gave 100 acres in Harrow, Herefrething Land, Wembley and Yeading, to Wulfred, Archbishop of Canterbury, in reparation for lands seized from the archbishop by her father. She added four more acres in compensation for her tardiness in handing over the landbooks associated with the property. Wulfred let the land to his kinsman, Werhard and he, in his will (*c*.832-45), restored it to Christchurch, Canterbury. The gift to Canterbury probably included some land at Roxeth acquired by Werhard about 845. Yeading was later attached to Hayes, the archbishop's other Middlesex property, but otherwise the boundaries of Harrow were probably already set.[9] Harrow had passed into the hands of Leofwin Godwinson, brother of King Harold, before 1066, but returned to the ownership of the Archbishop of Canterbury, before the Domesday Survey was made in 1086. The archbishops stayed in possession until Archbishop Cranmer was obliged to exchange it with Henry VIII in 1545.

THE DOMESDAY SURVEY 1086

The Domesday entry[10] for Harrow gives the following information:

Lanfranc, Archbishop of Canterbury owned it.

It was assessed for 100 hides.

There was arable land for 70 ploughs, but there were only 49 ploughs on the manor in 1086.

(The lord's demesne of 30 hides had 4 ploughs, but could have 5 more and the Frenchmen and villagers between them had 45 ploughs, but could have 16 more.)

A priest had 1 hide (120 acres).

3 knights had 6 hides and under them dwelt 7 men (presumably working the 6 hides)

13 villagers had half a hide (60 acres) each.

28 villagers had a virgate (quarter hide or 30 acres) each.

48 villagers had half a virgate (15 acres) each.

13 villagers had 4 hides between them.

2 cottagers had 13 acres between them.

There were 2 slaves.

There was an unspecified amount of pasture for village cattle.

There was woodland for 2000 pigs.

In the time of Edward the Confessor the manor had been worth £60.

When acquired by Archbishop Lanfranc it was worth £20.

In 1086 it was worth £56.

Earl Leofwin was the owner on the day when Edward was alive, and was dead.

Harrow's 100 hides were essentially units for tax assessment and did not necessarily equate

7. *Domesday Book 1086: The entry for Harrow.*

with 100 times 120 acres, but it must be said that medieval Harrow very likely did cover about 12,000 acres – nineteenth-century census returns give the area as 13,809 acres. On the other hand the hides and virgates given as belonging to the people of Harrow were actual areas and although a hide is usually accepted as being about 120 acres, there are regional variations and it appears from later documents (pp 35) that the Harrow hide was only 75 acres.

THE LAND
Information about the land is sparse. Woodland in Middlesex, Herts, Bucks, Beds and Cambridgeshire was measured by the Domesday Commissioners in terms of the number of pigs it would support. This suggests that such woodland was composed of oak or beech. The ancient forest believed to have covered most of Middlesex at an earlier period, but largely cleared for ploughland by 1086, was almost certainly oak and by the later medieval period had a hornbeam underlayer as well. It was the oak which supplied acorns for the pigs to forage among which counted in 1086. Domesday Book shows that all the manors along the hilly northern boundary of Middlesex were heavily wooded compared with those on the flatter lands further south. Whether this was simply because clearance was easier on the flat lands or due to the desire of early settlers to keep a wooded barrier between themselves and other groups to the north is uncertain. In any event the wooded part of

Harrow was almost certainly the northern part of Pinner and the Weald, an Old English name meaning woodland. The pasture for cattle may have been former woodland reduced to scrubland by grazing.

Although several brooks run towards the River Brent, and the River Pinn rises in Harrow Weald and flows through the Pinner portion of the manor, there was no reference to meadow which is usually found along the banks of waterways where they overflow. The streams were small and no important river runs through Harrow, which may account for the absence of any mills or fishponds.

THE PEOPLE
One hundred and seventeen people are listed as holding land in Harrow under the archbishop. The three knights, who were presumably Frenchmen, may not have lived on their estate. The two slaves would have been part of someone else's household. If these five are subtracted we are left with 112 heads of households in Harrow in 1086. If the average household at the time is assumed to be 4.5 there would have been a total population of about 504.

The main question is where did they live? None of the hamlets which made up medieval Harrow appear in the Domesday Book and the only ones to be recorded before 1086, were Wembley and Roxeth. Surely the 112 households were scattered about Harrow, already forming the nucleus of the 12 hamlets which had all emerged with distinct identities by the thirteenth century.

[1] Cotton, J: 'A Late Bronze Age Barbed Spearhead and Associated Finds from Park Wood, Ruislip'. *Transactions London & Middlesex Archaeological Society* 37 (1986).

[2] Cotton and Merriman, 'Some recent prehistoric finds from Greater London', *TLAMAS* 41 (1991)

[3] Cotton and Wood: 'Recent prehistoric finds from the Thames foreshore and beyond in Greater London', *TLAMAS* 47 (1996).

[4] Ellis, R: 'Excavations in Grim's Dyke, Harrow' *TLAMAS* 33 (1982).

[5] Seeley, F and Thorogood, C: 'Back to Brockley Hill' *London Archaeologist*, Vol 7, No 9 (1994).

[6] *Victoria History of the Counties of England, Middlesex* I, ed Cockburn, J S, King, H P F & McDonnell, K G T, (1969).

[7] Bushell, W D: *Harrow Octocentenary Tracts*, I, Early Charters (1883).

[8] Clarke, Patricia A: 'Anglo-Saxon Harrow and Hayes', *TLAMAS* 40 (1989).

[9] *Ibid.*

[10] *VCH op. cit* (1969).

Harrow and its Manors

HARROW OR SUDBURY MANOR

The Archbishop of Canterbury had manorial jurisdiction over the whole of Harrow, but within the bounds of the main manor were several other estates of manorial status, whose lords were obliged to attend the archbishop's court. These were the Rectory manor, in existence by 1233; Woodhall manor in Pinner, mentioned in a Lambeth Palace estate document of 1236; Headstone manor in Pinner, conveyed to the archbishop in 1344; Roxeth manor; Uxendon manor, Wembley manor and Tokyngton manor. Archbishops of Canterbury retained Harrow until December 1545 when Cranmer was obliged to hand it over to Henry VIII, who sold it in January 1546 to Sir Edward North, Chancellor of the Court of Augmentations. He became Lord North of Kirtling in 1554 and died ten years later. Dudley, third Baron North, who was said by Camden to have 'consumed the greater part of his estate in the gallantries of King James's court', repaired his losses in 1630 by selling Harrow to Edmund Phillips and George and Rowland Pitt. By 1636 George Pitt was in sole possession and his granddaughter Alice succeeded to the property in 1666. Her second husband was Sir James Rushout and their heirs inherited. The Rushouts

9. Thomas Cranmer, the last Archbishop of Canterbury to own the Manor of Harrow.

were created Barons Northwick in 1797. The widow of the third Lord Northwick (died 1887) began to sell the estate. Her grandson through an earlier marriage, Captain E.G. Spencer-Churchill, inherited in 1912 and sold the remainder in the 1920s, but retained the title of lord of the manor until his death in 1964.

MANOR COURTS

The power of lords of manors was exemplified in the courts which were held in their names. The archbishop had the right to hold a CourtLeet or View of Frankpledge which tried minor offences and dealt with breaches of the peace, as well as the Court Baron where changes in ownership of property were ratified and the working of the common fields was regulated. The quaint sounding name, 'Frankpledge' refers to the system descended from Saxon times whereby the men of each vill were divided into tithings. All males aged over 12 were obliged to join a tithing (notionally of ten men), which was a group responsible for the mutual good behaviour of its members. After the Norman Conquest

8. Estates of manorial status in Harrow.

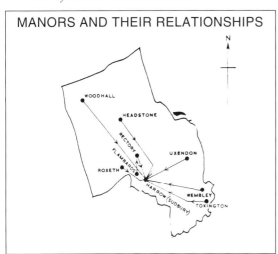

MANORS AND THEIR RELATIONSHIPS

10. Sir Edward North who purchased the Manor of Harrow from Henry VIII in January 1546.

the tithings were 'viewed' or inspected at a special session of the Hundred Court attended by the sheriff, but by the fourteenth century this took place at the Court Leet. In practice the two courts, Leet and Baron, often followed each other on the same day.

The liberties which the archbishop enjoyed in Harrow – granted, confirmed and enlarged by various medieval kings – allowed him certain financial privileges. Should, for example, the archbishop's men be tried and found guilty in a royal court and fined, the money or any forfeited goods were handed over to the archbishop. When Nicholas Brembre, mayor of London and lord of the manors of Roxeth and Uxendon (not to mention Northolt and Down Barnes outside Harrow) was attainted and executed in 1388, his property reverted to the Crown, but the archbishop got back Roxeth some years later. Also the archbishop's tenants were exempted from the duty of attending the court of the Hundred of Gore, the division of the county of Middlesex in which Harrow was situated. In medieval times this open-air court met about once a month

at Kingsbury where the Police Cadet training college now stands. The Hundred courts gradually lost importance and ceased to be held, but the Hundred was still in use for the administration of the militia until the First World War.

The court rolls and books of the manor of Harrow have been preserved in an almost unbroken series from 1315 to 1913. They show that courts were held nine or ten times a year in the fourteenth century, but only once or twice a year in the seventeenth century, usually about Easter and Michaelmas (29 September). There are occasional records of a court being held in an unusual place, such as Weald Wood in 1316 and at Roxeth in 1529. Otherwise the courts seem to have been held at the manor house in Sudbury, known as Sudbury Court for that reason. Once the separate Rectory manor had been established in the thirteenth century, the main manor became known as Sudbury manor to distinguish between the two.

The court rolls show that the tithings within Harrow corresponded with the hamlets. In the early fourteenth century each tithing was represented at the manor court by chief pledges, three for the large hamlet of Pinner, two each for Harrow Weald, Roxeth, Sudbury and Wembley and one each for Preston and Kenton. Alperton, Uxendon, Hatch End and Greenhill were sometimes tithings in their own right, but by the sixteenth century had been subsumed in other tithings. Aletasters who would assess the quality of ale sold and constables to preserve the peace in the various areas were appointed by the court. Other officials were beadles who collected the fines and other perquisites of the court and reeves who gathered in the rents and presented them for audit.

Representatives of the sub-manors were obliged to attend the manor court and could be fined if they defaulted.

THE MANOR HOUSE

Sudbury Court was the manor house and was where the archbishop lodged on his infrequent visits to Harrow, until Archbishop John Stratford built a grand new house at Headstone in the 1340s (see below). The old house included a chapel and there are references to ordinations having taken place there in the fourteenth century. Sudbury Court farmhouse in Sudbury Court Road, which was demolished in 1958, is believed to have been near the site of the archbishop's

11. *Su'dbury Court Farmhouse, which dated from the seventeenth century, is thought to have been near the site of the Archbishop of Canterbury's medieval manor house. The farmhouse was demolished in 1958.*

residence. It dated from the seventeenth century, but had a cellar of earlier date. There was one room called the court room as the manor courts continued to be held at Sudbury after the archbishops took themselves off to Headstone. Sudbury Court, let as a farm by later lords of the manor, was farmed by the Hill and Green families in the nineteenth century and by the Perrins until 1956, when it was sold for building.

THE RECTORY MANOR

The Rectory manor arose out of the hide of land recorded for the priest in the Domesday Survey. It was defined in 1233-40 as the demesne of the church, and gave the rector manorial jurisdiction over Harrow-on-the-Hill, part of Roxeth and the land over to and including part of Greenhill. The Rectory at which the courts were held was on the site of the house called The Grove at the top of Grove Hill, now part of Harrow School. The court rolls and books of the Rectory manor have also been well preserved, the rolls from 1329-1678 and the books from 1629-1896. The courts were held less frequently than in the main manor, only once a year in the fourteenth century, up to seven times a year in the fifteenth century, reverting to once or twice a year thereafter.

FLAMBARDS

An estate which took its name from a family called Flambard in the fourteenth century was a sub-manor of the Rectory manor. It belonged at different times to the Frowyks, the Gerards and the ubiquitous Richard Page. The house, which stood in London Road on the site of Nos. 27-41, was 'beautified' by Sir Gilbert Gerard between 1619-39 at a cost of some £3000 and was taxed for containing 25 hearths in 1664. Sadly it is believed to have degenerated into farm buildings and to have vanished in the late nineteenth century. An eighteenth-century house on the High Street is called Flambards and may have been a replacement. Richard Page began a new mansion further north which was finished by Lord Northwick who came into possession in 1807. He named it Harrow Park (or Villa) and filled it with splendid furnishings and the works of Italian masters such as Raphael and Titian, but seems to have let it rather than lived in it himself. It was sold to Major General Alexander Murray McGregor in 1825. The property was mortgaged and then bought by a master at Harrow School, the Revd W.W. Phelps, who converted it into a school boarding house. The Harrow Park Trust bought it in 1885 and it is still a boarding house, but houses were built on some of the ground.

12. *The ancient Flambards disappeared in 1884 when Manor Lodge was built; 27-41 London Road is now on the site. The eighteenth century house on the right of this print is called Flambards and may have replaced the old house. The wall of Harrow Park can be seen immediately on the right.*

WOODHALL AND HEADSTONE MANORS

These two manors in Pinner, along with Pinner Park, a medieval deer park enclosed by a bank and double ditch, were estates within the Archbishop of Canterbury's demesne (the land retained for the lord of the manor's own use, although frequently let out on lease). As early as 1236 there was a grange at Woodhall and 312 acres of land which must have been cleared from the surrounding woodland and lay between Pinner Wood and the Uxbridge Road. A grange was a manorial outpost, particularly when the manor belonged to a monastery. The grange, which may have been a simple building used for

to William Pennifather of Northolt manor who was a grocer, citizen and Lord Mayor of London, but the manorial rights were joined to Sudbury manor. Woodhall Farm passed through various hands and was part of A.W. Tooke's Pinner Hill Estate by 1864. No court rolls or court books have survived, if indeed any courts were ever held.

There is no evidence of courts having been held for Headstone manor either. The property was granted to the Archbishop of Canterbury in 1344 by Robert Wodehouse, Treasurer of the Exchequer and Archdeacon of Richmond. It consisted of a house and about 200 acres. The archbishops lost it along with the rest of Harrow in 1546 and the manorial rights of Headstone stayed with Sir Edward North and his successors, but the house and land was sold in 1630 to Simon Rewse who was already leasing it and living there. One of Simon's sons, Francis, was fined by Parliament for his part in supporting Charles I during the Civil War and maybe because he needed cash, he sold Headstone to William Williams in 1649, who kept it until selling it to Sir William Bucknall in 1671. His family retained it until Victorian times. Headstone Farm, as it was then known, had 412 acres at the time of the 1851 census, when John Hill, the tenant farmer employed 14 labourers there. The name changed to Moat Farm at the beginning of the

13. *Coade stone lion at Harrow Park, moved from the garden door in 1906.*

storage of implements and produce rather than a dwelling, was apparently replaced by a farmhouse in Tudor times and was rebuilt early in the nineteenth century and is now Woodhall Farm in Woodhall Drive.

The ownership of Woodhall went with the main manor until 1630, when the farm was sold

14. Headstone Manor - the eastern elevation c.1972.

twentieth century. Edward York sold the manor house and 63 acres of land to Hendon Rural District Council in 1925 for recreational purposes. By the 1970s the house was in some danger as it was simply occupied by the head groundsman and the barn was in sad need of restoration. The barn was repaired in 1973 by the council, but not used for anything. A Harrow Museum Group was formed in 1981 and after enormous voluntary effort the Harrow Arts and Heritage Trust was set up in 1985 and the barn was opened in 1986 to display museum material and provide a venue for arts activities. Some rooms in the house are also open to the public and work continues on the restoration of the house and expansion of the museum.

15. Harrow Park in 1881. This house was begun by Richard Page in the eighteenth century and completed by Lord Northwick after 1807.

16. Woodhall Farm, now a private house, which is on the site of the Archbishop of Canterbury's Woodhall grange.

17. Headstone Manor and barn. The manor belonged to the Archbishop of Canterbury from 1344-1546. Portions of the fourteenth-century house lurk behind the eighteenth-century facade. The barn was built in 1506.

THE MOATED MANOR HOUSE

The Headstone estate had belonged to the de la Hegge family in the thirteenth century and took its name, Heggeston, later metamorphosed into Headstone, from them. The archbishop in 1344, John Stratford, seems to have made Headstone his principal dwelling in Harrow and he is credited with having built a new house within a moat. Though probably contemporary with Stratford's house, the date of the moat is unknown, but it was a fashionable and costly status symbol, with practical uses; providing water, sew-

18. Headstone Barn after restoration in 1973.

19. *This picture, dated 1766, shows The Grove standing out from the trees to the right of the church. It is on the site of the Rectory Manor House. It became a school house in the 1820s and, having been severely damaged by fire in 1833, was largely rebuilt.*

age, a breeding place for fish and an obstacle to keep animals out of the gardens and living quarters. The moat, which remains complete at Headstone, was consistent with the archbishop's wealth and position. Despite the centuries which have elapsed since its erection a portion of the great hall and small rooms on the other side of the cross passage survive from Stratford's timber-framed house. All the other medieval buildings, the chapel where Simon Langham ordained several men in 1367, a gatehouse, stables, barn and dovecote, have all gone. The great barn that is now the museum was built in 1506 and there is a smaller barn, damaged by fire in 1978, which was probably built at the same time.

The splendid house must have been used on relatively few occasions by the archbishops as their ecclesiastical and public duties as well as the care of their other estates must have left them with little leisure to visit Harrow. From the 1380s Headstone was let out to tenants who were, from 1397 to 1545, always members of the Redyng family. The leases normally required the tenant to have rooms and stabling ready for the archbishops and their retainers. The house when used by the archbishops must have been for private purposes such as entertaining or rest and recuperation. Pinner Park with its deer was close by.

From the time that Sir Edward North took over the lordship of Harrow, Headstone degenerated into a rather superior farmhouse. The Rewses, Williams's and Bucknalls altered the house to make it comfortable according to the standards of their day. The great hall was ceiled, walls were panelled, extensions built at different times and the rooms were remodelled and the front was given a brick facade in 1772. At first glance this medieval house appears to date from the eighteenth century.

WEMBLEY, UXENDON AND TOKYNGTON MANORS

These three manors on the eastern edge of Harrow all came into the hands of the Page family in the sixteenth and seventeenth centuries. The Priory of Kilburn owned an estate in Wembley, Tokyngton and Alperton from the thirteenth century and the prioress held courts at Wembley before Kilburn Priory was dissolved in 1536. Richard Page, who leased Sudbury Court, acquired Wembley manor in 1542 and the family

20. *The Great Barn at Roxeth in 1947, the year before it was demolished. It stood within a moat. The associated medieval manor house had already gone before 1547.*

remained in possession until 1802-4, at which time part was sold to Samuel Hoare, the banker and part to John Gray. Sir Edward Watkin of the Metropolitan Railway Company bought the estate in 1862 and it became Wembley Park. The manor house was on the south side of Wembley Green, but was rebuilt by John Gray in 1810 and demolished in 1908. Some court rolls survive for 1781 and 1795.

Uxendon, named as a manor in 1373, having been taken by the Crown at the time of Nicholas Brembre's execution, was sold to Thomas Goodlake, a London merchant, and then passed by marriage to the Boys family in the early fifteenth century and to the Bellamys, also by marriage, a century later. The Bellamys were Roman Catholics who suffered greatly for sheltering priests at Uxendon in the late sixteenth century. Two were executed, some died in prison and others went into exile. Those who survived were financially ruined by fines for not attending church, so that the Uxendon property was heavily mortgaged and passed to Richard Page in 1609. It remained with the Pages until 1829. The main settlement at Uxendon was at Forty Green. The manor house was later known as Uxendon Farm and was rebuilt in the nineteenth century. It became the Lancaster Shooting Club in 1900 and ended its days under the railway line from Wembley Park to Stanmore which opened in 1932. Only one court roll survives, for the year 1608.

Tokyngton manor, a freehold estate of the Barnville family at the end of the thirteenth century, was never under the lordship of the Archbishop of Canterbury. It included a chapel at Tokyngton and was interspersed with the Priory of Kilburn's lands. Like Uxendon it was owned by the Bellamys in the sixteenth century

and was acquired by Richard Page in 1609. Although the estate was referred to as a manor in 1505, no court rolls or books have survived. The manor house was used as a farmhouse. approached from lodges in Wembley Hill Road and Harrow Road in Victorian times. From 1862-83 it became the home of Lord Derby's daughter and son-in-law, when it was called Oakington Park. Later it was known as Sherren's Farm. The house and land were conveyed to Wembley Urban District Council in 1938 to be public open space. The ARP blew up the house and set it on fire in 1939 as an exercise!

ROXETH MANOR

Roxeth, lying south-west of the hill and Lower Road, came into the hands of the Archbishops of Canterbury about 1370 when the owner of the freehold property, William Roxeth, was outlawed and his land (166 acres bringing in 45 shillings rent) was taken by the lord of the manor. It was granted to the unlucky Nicholas Brembre and after his execution, eventually regained by the archbishops. It then passed with the main manor until 1630, when the farm along with Pinner Park was sold to Thomas Hutchinson and his son, John, while the manorial rights remained with the lords of Sudbury Manor. In 1678 John Hutchinson sold Roxeth Place to Thomas Smith and Robert Nichols and by 1727 it belonged to Thomas Brian, headmaster of Harrow School. Mr Chapman, a local builder who erected some of the new buildings at the school, built a house called Roxeth Grange which became Grange Farm. He is described as builder and farmer of 100 acres in the 1851 census. The moated site of the medieval manor house lay within the grounds. The Halls were the farmers around the beginning of the twentieth century and had model cow houses there in 1909. Members of the same family have been running Pinner Park Farm as a dairy farm since 1924.

The moated manor house which had been situated near the junction of Northolt Road and Roxeth Hill, had disappeared by 1547, although part of the moat and the great barn survived until 1948. The barn was damaged by fire bombs during the war and because of insufficient local interest in its preservation, it was demolished in 1948. The farm was sold for development in 1962 and the Grange Farm estate was built there in 1969.

Source: *Victoria County History, Middlesex*, Vol IV

St Mary's Church

The physical feature which marks out Harrow for miles around is the steeple of St Mary's church on top of the hill. The fact that a priest is mentioned in the Domesday Survey suggests that a church was already established in Harrow by 1086 and it is probably safe to assume that a heathen temple had been rebuilt or converted to christian worship at a much earlier date, possibly by Abbot Stidberht in the eighth century or by the priest, Werhard to whom Archbishop Wulfred granted Harrow for life before 845. Lanfranc, Archbishop of Canterbury (1070-89), who rebuilt Canterbury Cathedral in Norman style and instigated other ecclesiastical building, was responsible for a new church being built in his manor of Harrow. Being incomplete at the time of his death it fell to his successor

at Canterbury, Anselm, to consecrate it in 1094. Anselm's right to do so was challenged by Maurice, Bishop of London, in whose diocese Harrow is situated and his representative tried to steal the holy oils to prevent the ceremony from taking place. The story goes that the thief was bewildered by the roads around the hill and simply went round in circles, ending up back at the church, where the oils were retrieved and the consecration was carried out. The question of who should have jurisdiction over Harrow church, the Archbishop of Canterbury or the Bishop of London, was settled when Bishop Wulfstan of Worcester, the last surviving pre-conquest bishop, supported the archbishop's claim. Harrow was a 'peculiar' of the Archbishop of Canterbury within the Deanery of Croydon until 1845, when all the Middlesex peculiars were abolished and it became part of the diocese of London.

Although presumably of a grand design in

21. The 'Church Visible'. This view of London c.1690 suggests that 'Horowe on the hill' with its steepled church and the town spilling down the slope, was a landmark from as far away as Southwark.

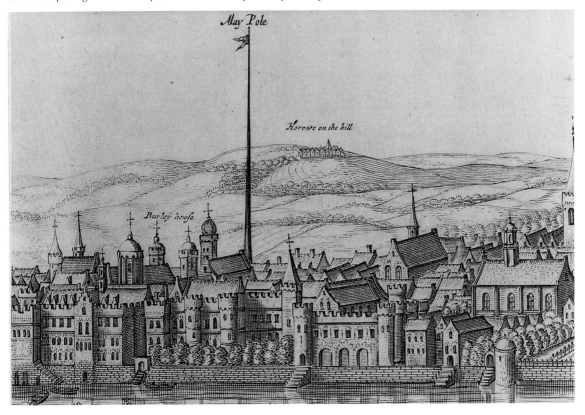

keeping with its illustrious owner, Lanfranc's building survived for a relatively short time. The bottom part of the tower of the present church is the only possible remnant of Lanfranc's building and this is open to discussion as the late Norman west doorway set into it dates from *c*.1140 and the whole tower may have been first built at that time. Another question is whether this Norman church had an apse or a chancel at the east end.

REBUILDING

There is no evidence of a rebuilding of the church as a whole until a century later when fashions had changed and Elias of Dereham, rector 1205-50, built or rebuilt the chancel and probably the nave in Early English style. Elias was also a canon of Salisbury Cathedral which was being built at the same period and he had a great interest in architecture and influence on that and other important buildings. The transepts at Harrow were added a little later, probably about 1300, which would have been while Ralph de Knovill was rector. Edward I came to Harrow

23. St Mary's before Sir Gilbert Scott added his battlements and refaced the wall with knapped flint during the restoration of 1846-9.

several times around that time and archbishop's visits are recorded as well. It is possible that gifts from these personages or simply the need to accommodate their retinues, led to the expansion.

The last major alterations, which gave the church a perpendicular appearance took place about 1450, when John Byrkhede, another master builder, was rector. He was a friend of Archbishop Chichele and was buried at Harrow in 1468, his memorial brass being in the chancel. A clerestory was added to heighten and lighten the nave. This necessitated a new roof, which remains in place with its apostles standing under canopies carved on the wall posts supporting the tie beams, reminding us of the dedication and skill of the fifteenth-century craftsmen. At the same time matching perpendicular windows replaced the lancets in the nave aisles and a south porch was built, which has a small room or parvis on top, which may have been used as living quarters for a priest. The upper storey of the tower was rebuilt and then or a little later, crowned by the noble octagonal spire. Middlesex cannot compete with counties such as Somerset and Suffolk for its churches and the glory of Harrow spire depends upon its position as much as its architecture, but it is an awe-inspiring sight and as Charles II remarked, a perfect example of the *church visible*. It is a view of which later generations were nearly deprived, for the steeple was struck by lightning in 1765 and had to be partially rebuilt. A further disaster was averted in September 1815, when plumbers who were soldering the lead, went to dinner, leaving

22. The twelfth-century font of Purbeck marble spent the years from 1801 to 1842 as a rather splendid ornamental plant pot in a Harrow garden.

24. *Carving on the fifteenth-century roof.*

their stove with a fire in it and the woodwork was set alight. Fortunately the fire was spotted by a passer-by and extinguished by pails of water.

By the late eighteenth century the church was dilapidated and neglected. A visitor who wrote to the *Gentleman's Magazine* about it in 1786, claimed that the chancel was so ruinous as to be dangerous to enter, with cracks in the walls, not one whole pane of glass and the east window propped up to prevent its falling. A local inhabitant to whom he had spoken had attributed this state of affairs to an argument between the lord of the manor and the person leasing the rectory. There had indeed been such a dispute a century earlier between George Pitt who was both lord of the manor and lay rector and Sir Gilbert Gerard who leased the rectorial tithes, as to who should repair the chancel, normally the responsibility of the rector. Although settled, the quarrel broke out afresh in the 1780s and again in the nineteenth century. However, neglect of churches seems to have been common at that time.

The church owes its present appearance to George Gilbert Scott who undertook its restoration between 1846-9. He added a north chapel, rebuilt the north porch and the top part of the south porch and remodelled the chancel. He added battlements to the clerestory, aisles, porches and transepts. The exterior walls were refaced in neat knapped flints, except for the tower which is rendered with plaster and pebble dashed. Since then vestries have been built onto the north chapel in 1909 and a hall in 1960.

25. *The noble spire was added to the tower shortly after 1450. This photograph was taken from Church Fields in 1928.*

THE INTERIOR

Changes to the inside of the church have largely followed the varying patterns of worship since the Reformation. Henry VIII's policy of suppressing monasteries and seizing their wealth was extended in 1545 (by which time there were no religious houses left) to chantries, fraternities, guilds and free chapels. The work was carried out at the beginning of Edward VI's reign when the confiscation of valuables belonging to parish churches was planned as well. There was a chantry at Harrow, founded by William de Bosco who was rector 1312-24. A chantry consisted of a special altar set up in a convenient space in the church at which a daily mass was said for the repose of the soul of the founder, by a priest who was supported by an endowment. William de Bosco's chantry was handsomely endowed for he left a property in Kenton with land amounting to 100 acres, houses in the High Street at Harrow, a field and wood at Watford and a chantry house and land at Hatch End in the area of the modern Chantry Road and Chantry Place, for that purpose. The priest would have been able to live in or let the chantry house. The churchwardens told the commissioners inquiring into the value of chantries etc in 1548 that it was then worth £9 12s 1d per year. Having been confiscated, all the chantry property was sold to William Gyes of the Strand for £747 8s 6d and ceased to have any connection with the church.

An inventory of 'all the goods plate, ornaments, jewels and bells belonging and appertaining to the church of Harrow'[1] taken in 1549 was certified before a jury on 3 August 1552. The intention was that each church should be left with the minimum amount of plate necessary for use at services, all the rest being sent to the Jewel House in the Tower of London to be melted down for the king's use. Vestments and poorer quality plate could be sold locally and altar linen should be given to the poor. Altars had been ordered to be removed from churches in 1551. They were to be replaced with tables usually situated in the nave, rather than the sanctuary. William Page and John Perser, the churchwardens that year, listed a silver and gilt chalice and a great and a little pyx, each of silver, for covering the sacrament, to be retained at the church and stated that the parishioners had agreed to sell a silver cross, a silver chalice and a silver censor. They were bought by John Coke, a London goldsmith for £24 13s. Latten, copper and pewter goods had been sold the previous year for £7 16s. The cloth and hangings associated with the rood, the crucifix between figures of Our Lady and Saint John which had hung above the rood screen, brought in 3 shillings. The screen and rood would probably have been swept away from their position at the entrance to the chancel about this time. There was also a list of altar coverings and vestments and further lists of linen and vestments stolen from the church in 1551 and 1552. Bearing in mind that from henceforth sermons would be of supreme importance in religious services a new pulpit had been purchased for less than £3. The roof leads had been repaired and the windows reglazed. Whether or not this was because stained glass had been removed is uncertain.

By the beginning of the nineteenth century the nave was filled with box pews, and there was a gallery above the north aisle where the boys from Harrow School sat in the years before the first school chapel was built (1839). A reredos obscured much of the east window and a three-decker pulpit, given to the church by Tanner Arnold esq in 1708, dominated the nave. George Gilbert Scott replaced the old east window with one of 'decorated' style and removed the reredos. The sounding board and reading desk were removed from the pulpit, making it fit more comfortably into the background. Unfortunately a new sounding board was placed above it in 1910. The galleries were renewed, but have since been taken away. In 1894 some of the stonework of the lancet windows in the chancel which predated Elias Dereham's remodelling *c.*1250, were rediscovered and restored. They are filled with glass by Kempe and Tower, depicting the five joyful mysteries of the Blessed Virgin Mary. The glass in the clerestory windows dates from

26. The interior of the church about 1900. Sir Gilbert Scott put in the Decorated style east window.

1902 and tells the story of the church and school.

There are ten monumental brasses dating from 1370 (Sir Edmund Flambard and his wife) to 1613, including one to John Lyon, the founder of Harrow School, and his wife, Joan. There is also a memorial to John Lyon, by Flaxman, erected in 1813.

TOKYNGTON CHAPEL

In 1548 the churchwardens explained that there was a free chapel at Tokyngton, within the parish of Harrow, which had been endowed with land and tenements but 'by whom, how long time past or to what use it was founded the said parson and churchwardens know not'. The last priest, William Layton, had already surrendered the chapel to the Crown in 1545 and it was suppressed along with other chantries and free chapels. This chapel, dedicated to St Michael, which served the communities of Wembley Green and Tokyngton, was mentioned for the first time about 1240 and a priest called Benedict was named in a charter as being the rector there in the 1270s. After the closure the property was leased several times, coming into the hands of the Page family in 1607. The old chapel buildings had been destroyed before Daniel Lysons wrote his *Environs of London* in 1798. The site was on the south side of South Way beside Wembley Hill Station. The modern church of St Michael, Tokyngton, opened in 1933, reminds posterity of its lost predecessor.

27. An almost certainly fanciful view of Tokyngton Chapel, by Chatelain, published in 1751.

PINNER CHURCH

The populous hamlet of Pinner had its own chapel by 1234, which was probably rebuilt before being consecrated by Peter, the Bishop of Corbavia in 1321. It was usually served from Harrow, but had its own ministers for much of the seventeenth century and eventually became independent of the mother church in 1766.

BENTLEY PRIORY

A small priory, dependent upon St Gregory's at Canterbury, was established in Harrow Weald before 1248, in which year the chronicler, Matthew Paris, related the sad tale of the prior of Bentley being suffocated when a heap of grain of which he was accessing the value, collapsed. The Harrow manor court rolls in 1512 explain that an Archbishop of Canterbury had given Bentley to St Gregory's 'time out of mind' and complain that no canon had been presented to Bentley for 20 years past and no priest had said mass there for two years. Since Lanfranc had founded St Gregory's, he probably made the endowment. The priory was not suppressed at the time of the Reformation, suggesting that it was no longer in existence in the 1530s. The old priory is believed to have been near Lower Priory Farm in Clamp Hill, Harrow Weald.

THE HERMITAGE

A hermitage dedicated to St Edmund and St Catherine stood on Sudbury Common, but had ceased to fulfil its original function by 1529, when it was said to have been in the lord's hands for many years past. A property of the same name became part of the Flambards estate. It is shown on Rocque's map of 1754 (see page 6). A late nineteenth-century house now stands on the site. From 1898 the Revd W. Done Bushell, a housemaster at Harrow School, lived there during his retirement. The Bowden House Psychiatric Clinic (St Andrew's) moved there from Sudbury Hill House in 1926.

28. St John the Baptist's, Pinner, was consecrated in 1321 and became a parish in its own right in 1766.

29. Hermitage and Little House, built as a single house in the 1830s, called Woodside Cottage. The old Hermitage lay behind. Bowden House Psychiatric Clinic moved there in 1926.

RECTORS

The rector of a parish was normally responsible for the spiritual welfare of the inhabitants and derived an income from his glebeland and the tithes (tenths of their produce, stock and labour) given to him by the parishioners. Should a rector be a person with duties elsewhere, there was usually some provision made for a vicar (meaning deputy) to work in the parish on the rector's behalf. Frequently a vicar had some of the glebeland and the tithes were divided into the great tithes of corn, hay and wood which went to the rector, and the small tithes of milk, eggs etc which were collected by the vicar. Rectors were normally responsible for the upkeep of the chancel of the church, the part where the altar stood. The right to present someone to a rectory or vicarage is known as the advowson.

The Archbishops of Canterbury had the advowson of Harrow rectory until 1544. On the few occasions when a new rector was needed when the archbishopric was vacant, the Crown took over the appointment. When the king, Henry II, put in his own man in 1170, the turbulent archbishop, Thomas Becket, promptly excommunicated the unlucky rector. Those who became rectors of so prestigious a place were generally men who had already distinguished themselves in ecclesiastical affairs and held other offices. Dr Thomas Wilkinson, rector 1471-78, was also a dean of St Paul's, an archdeacon of Canterbury and prebendary of Tottenham, while William Bolton in the 1520s was prior of St Bartholomew's at Smithfield. Although many may have regarded Harrow as a source of income and a rural retreat, others like Elias de Dereham and John Byrkhede clearly lavished care and attention on the church and spent much time at the rectory house.

The rectors held the hide of land which had belonged to the Domesday priest and a rectory house close to the church, thought to be on the site of the house called The Grove which has been a boarding house of Harrow School since *c*.1820. This made up the Rectory manor. In return they owed suit of court at the Sudbury manor court and paid 8 shillings per annum rent and a heriot (death duty) at the appropriate time. A new house was built by Prior Bolton in 1524, because he feared that the Thames was going to burst its banks and flood the whole of London as predicted by a fortune-teller and wanted a fortress on the hill, or so the story goes. John Stow in *The Survey of London* written in 1598

30. *The so-called Prior Bolton's Ark. It was a folly in the grounds of The Mount (St Dominic's convent). It was built c.1820 upon Tudor foundations and was demolished in 1968.*

31. The photographer seems to have been standing on the church tower. The building beside the lych gate is the vicarage. The present building dates from 1870, but a vicarage has occupied this site since c1233.

discounts this tale and says that Bolton simply repaired the parsonage (another word for rectory is parsonage) and only built a dove house. The house which was leased out by later rectors who were laymen after the Reformation, became simply a gentleman's country house and Richard Brinsley Sheridan, the politician and playwright, lived there 1781-4. A destructive fire led to its rebuilding in its present form in 1833.

Thomas Cranmer surrendered the advowson of the rectory to Henry VIII in November 1544 and it was granted to Christ Church, Oxford in 1546. The rector at the time, Richard Coxe, was also dean of Christ Church. The following year, the college retained the great tithes of Harrow, but transferred the rectory to Sir Edward North who had just become lord of Sudbury manor. He and his descendants had to pay the college £13 6s 8d per annum, but he would have the profits of the Rectory manor courts. In 1550 Sir Edward North obtained a 50-year lease on the parsonage and the great tithes, paying a further £74 17s 8d each year. However, the sixteenth century was a time of high inflation and perhaps because the college needed cash, Christ Church sold a 99-year lease of the parsonage and great tithes to

Nicholas Todd in 1566. This lease would have reverted to Todd when North's lease expired at the end of the century, had not he sold his interest to William Wightman in 1569. Endless complications ensued with North leasing the rectory, but not the right to hold manor courts, and subleasing the tithes to Wightman, who in turn subleased the Sudbury tithes to Sir Gilbert Gerard. After two law cases in 1593 the rectory and tithes were held separately from Christ Church. The Rectory manor stayed with North's descendants until being sold to George Pitt and others in 1630 and then passed to the Rushouts and Lord Northwick as did Sudbury manor. The great tithes were leased to various people ending with Richard Page at the time of the enclosure of the common fields in 1803, when tithes on enclosed land were extinguished. Corn-rents worth £1005 a year were substituted and Christ Church did extraordinarily well out of the allocation of land, receiving 897 acres in Preston, Alperton, Kenton, Harrow Weald and around Tithe Farm, Roxeth. This was far in excess of the value of the tithes. The estate was leased and sub-leased to farmers until finally being sold for building development, mainly in the 1920s and 30s.

VICARS

The rectors of Harrow had the right to appoint the vicars. The archbishop, Edmund Rich, endowed the vicarage 1233-40 while Elias of Dereham was rector. There was to be a house with the oblations of Harrow church and Tokyngton and Pinner chapels, the small tithes, the tithes of hay from Roxeth and Headstone manors and mortuaries of beasts worth less than 2 shillings. A mortuary was a death duty payable to the church, usually the second-best beast belonging to the dead person. The vicarage house was built just south of the churchyard. Towards the end of the eighteenth century the vicar lived in Pinner and let the vicarage to the school. In 1870 it was replaced by a new building, part of which is still used as a vicarage. The other section, called St Mary's House, is a Retreat House.

THE ANCIENT PARISH DIVIDED

Pinner became a Perpetual Curacy in 1766, the first of the hamlets to become independent of St Mary's. Churches were built in other areas during the nineteenth and twentieth century and new parishes developed as the population increased.

[1]PRO: E315/498

32. *The Peachey Tomb photographed about a hundred years ago. Byron, while a schoolboy at Harrow, used to loll on this gravestone to write poetry. The railings were added to prevent others from emulating him.*

Rural Harrow

MISDEMEANOURS

Nearly everything that we know about the people of Harrow before the seventeenth century comes from manorial documents, and gives us a rather dry and perhaps unbalanced view of their lives. We can find out how much rent they paid for their houses, what quantities of land they farmed and what services they were obliged to perform for the lord of the manor, but only a little about their recreations and domestic affairs. A perusal of the court rolls of any manor gives the impression that our ancestors spent most of their time in an untidy and possibly smelly landscape of broken-down fences, unmade hedgerows and filthy ditches, which they were too lazy to cleanse until they were threatened with a fine if the job were not done before a certain date. John Boys was presented by the tithing men of Weald on account of the state of his ditch at Rough Street in May 1416; one of many similar cases over the centuries.

During their spare time the men and women of Harrow seem to have quarrelled amongst themselves about property boundaries, or drank ale, which according to the aletasters (officials responsible for testing the quality and checking the measures) was sub standard. Joan Sextayne was fined 2d because she did not put up a sign outside her alehouse in 1462, but nothing was said about the quality of her ale. Occasionally one comes across someone like Peter Austin who, in 1501, varied what might otherwise have been a dull life, by standing under his neighbour's windows at night 'to hear the different words spoken, whereby divers strifes and discords have arisen among the neighbours'. He was fined 4d. Back in 1425 John Roxeth must have been doing much the same sort of thing, when he was presented at the manor court for being a common eavesdropper, 'prying by night into the secrets of his neighbours'.

These and other misdemeanours were dealt with at the Court Leet and were usually punished by a fine. The sums seem small, but if a labourer were earning 2d a day, a sixpenny fine would take half his week's wages. There is a good deal of variation in the levels of fines which may indicate that amounts were tailored to a person's means. John Ponder had to pay 6s 8d (a third of a pound) in 1430 because he disturbed

the court by litigating with John Janky and saying 'raca' to him, but Thomas Archer in 1456 was only fined 12d for what sounds like a similar offence, disturbing the court and saying 'raca' to his neighbours before the steward when sitting in court. Whatever can 'raca' have meant?

People were fined for failing to obtain a licence from the lord of the manor before giving their daughters in marriage. John Le Lyng, John Swetman and Matilda Le Yonge offended in this way in 1377. John Intowne who as a tenant of the Rectory Manor, probably dwelt in Harrow Town as his name suggests, sounds to have been ambitious for his son, William, sending him away to learn the liberal arts, but he had not obtained the lord's consent and an order was made, in 1384, that his goods should be seized. Two years later, the bailiff reported that he had taken a horse from him as a distress. If he were sufficiently wealthy to send his son to school, we must hope that he could stand the loss of a horse, which was probably valued at 6s 8d.

SPORT AND SOCIAL LIFE

Archery was practised at the butts and there are references in the court rolls to the butts being out of repair in 1505. Other remarks about sport or social activities are mostly negative in kind. Fishing in ponds, which may have been for food rather than sport, was forbidden. The catching of hares in nets was, however, allowed after the 23 April, when the breeding season was over, although other hunting was the privilege of the lord of the manor. Great efforts were made to prevent gambling. Robert Wynter and others were fined for allowing people to play at dice in their houses in 1517 and four years later, a chaplain, Robert Sowlle was fined for playing dice with two of John Lyon's servants. No wonder some Harrow men were reduced to listening under their neighbours' windows for amusement.

MANORIAL CUSTOMS

Manors were intended to increase the wealth of their lords and in medieval times the people of Harrow were tied to that manor and could not move elsewhere without the lord's licence, as the work which they were obliged to do by custom on the demesne (the lord's personal estate) was as much part of his assets as the rent which they paid. The customary works were commensurate with the size of land holdings. A survey of 1285

A View of the Shooting for the Silver Arrow, at Harrow the Hill.

Names of the Archers for 1769	And for 1770	Num.ʳ of Shoots.					Names of the Archers for 1769	And for 1770	Num.ʳ of Shoots.				
Mr. Whitmore	Mr. Lemon						Mr. Leigh	Mr. Lewis					
Mr. Lemon	Mr. Tighe						Mr. Tunstall	Rt. Hon. L.d Rawdon					
Mr. Maclean	Mr. Watkins						Mr. Jones	Mr. Franks					
Mr. Tighe	Mr. Leigh						Mr. Merry	Mr. Allen					
Mr. Watkins	Mr. Tunstall						Mr. Yalman	Mr. Crosbie					
Mr. Poyntz	Mr. Powell						Mr. Franks	Mr. Merry					

33. Archery became part of the life of Harrow School. Parents had to provide their sons with bows and arrows according to John Lyon's statutes of 1590. The scene depicted here is on a score card for the school's silver arrow competition in 1769-70

shows that the tenants of large tenements of one or one and a half hides worked for one day a week for the lord for 48 weeks of the year and performed 12 carting services a year as well in the main manor. There were also special boon days at ploughing and harvest times when extra work had to be done. Gradually the requirement to work a set number of days for the lord was replaced by the payment of a quit rent (to be quit of all services). Alfwin, son of Godmar of Pinner was already 'paying for all customs' as early as 1232 and by the time of the Black Death (1348-50), which speeded up the process of commuting work for money payment, nearly half the tenants had already done it. Some boon works lingered on into the sixteenth century. The lords of the manor or their lessees hired labourers to do the work after the customary services ceased.

There were other perquisites belonging to the lord of a manor. When a tenant died the lord could claim a heriot or death duty and when property passed from one generation to another

34. *Mr Curl and his sheep at Wealdstone Farm, Harrow Weald, at the beginning of the twentieth century. Sheep grazed Sudbury Common and Sudbury cotlanders paid 'a black sheep only' as a heriot or death duty in the sixteenth and seventeenth centuries.*

or was sold, a sum of money called a relief was payable to the lord. The various fines and other profits of court also went to the lord or to anyone to whom he might have leased out the rights.

The lord's rights and the tenants' duties arose through custom and were redefined from time to time. The customs of Harrow or Sudbury manor and the Rectory manor as 'time out of mind used by Dudley, Lord North', written in 1609, provide a useful insight into the workings of the manorial system in Harrow then, and probably for several centuries previously.[1] They are similar to the customs written down in a 1547 terrier (land survey).[2]

The customal relates to copyholders, whose titles to their property depended upon a copy of the entry made in the court roll when they took possession. There were also freehold tenants, like the Readings of Headstone, who usually held their estates by lease. According to this document there were three sorts of copyholders in Harrow: head tenants, undersetts and cotlanders.

The head tenants held a hide, a half-hide, or a yardland.

These measures of land are defined as:
one hide equals 100 lands or 100 selions;
a half hide equals 50 lands or 50 selions;
a yardland equals a quarter hide or 25 lands or 25 selions (i.e. a virgate);
a selion equals 3 roods or three quarters of an acre.

After this unusual precision the writer of the customal enters a caveat 'Howbeit every hide, half hide, yard land and selion of land doth not always contain a certain quantity of land, but is sometimes more and sometimes less, as the same has been time out of mind used and accustomed'. The hide in Harrow was apparently 75 acres (be it more or less!) rather than the more generally accepted 120 acres. This tallies quite closely with the neighbouring manor of Ruislip where it has been concluded from a sixteenth-century Terrier that a selion was slightly more than 3 roods, making an 80 acre hide.[3] Maybe the smaller hide was common on the heavy clay lands of north-west Middlesex. The selions were the strips of land in the open fields.

35. *These men happily fish in what seems to be a pond on private land, about 1800. In the sixteenth century fishing in ponds had been forbidden.*

The undersetts were parcels of a head tenement. They usually consisted of a cottage, garden and orchard and sometimes a small enclosure nearby. The head tenant was responsible for the services and customs of the ancient tenement, attending court, and paying a relief equivalent to one year's rent over and above the normal rent when he took possession, as well as the heriot. The undersetts were spared these customary dues to the lord of the manor, but had to pay the head tenants to whom they were underset the equivalent of a relief and 3s 6d as a death duty.[4]

Cotlanders were found only in the hamlet of Sudbury. There were 14 of them in the seventeenth century, but there had been 17 in the thirteenth century, and they had 5 acres or thereabouts each. Despite the small size of the holdings they were counted as head tenements and a heavy rent of 5 shillings per year was levied, 'which is greater rent than is answered to the lord for any other copyhold lands within the said manors'.[5] This works out at 9d per selion, whereas all other tenants paid an annual rent of 3d per selion. However, the Sudbury cotlanders were better off at the time of their deaths (or their heirs were) because all other head tenement holders had to pay as a heriot (death duty) 'the best cloven-footed beast... or mare or gelding', but the cotlanders' heriot was 'a black sheep only' and if they had no sheep, 10d. The heir of any head tenement who had no animals at the time of death, was permitted to pay 3s 6d as a 'dead' heriot, but if the head tenant had conveyed all his cattle to his children or anyone else 'with intent to defraud the lord' the heir could be refused admission to his land until a live animal had been handed over.[6]

MANORIAL OFFICIALS[7]

A reeve who was responsible for collecting the rents and a beadle to gather in the fines and other perquisites of the court, were chosen at Sudbury manor at the first court held after Michaelmas. Both officers were accountable at the lord's audit and received emoluments, 50 shillings a year for the reeve and 10 shillings for the beadle. Only one man was chosen for the Rectory manor which had fewer tenants, to act as both reeve and beadle. He was paid the odd sum of 5s 8d per year. Notwithstanding the recompense these positions were not popular as the lord could distrain the officials' lands if there was a shortfall in the accounts, but anyone elected by the homage at the manor court must serve or pay a fine. The tenants of Sudbury manor were to pay their rent twice yearly, at the feast of the Annunciation (25 March) and Michaelmas (29 September), those of the Rectory manor just once a year at Michaelmas.

There was also a bailiff who was accountable to the lord of the manor. His office was to serve any writs, warrants and processes from the sheriff of the county of Middlesex which had to be executed within the manor. He also seized felons' goods, stray animals and heriots. He received 40 shillings a year.

COPYHOLDERS' RIGHTS[8]

Copyholders who had inherited their property had a good deal of freedom over it, being allowed to pull down, sell, or carry away their houses. Timber-framed houses could be dismantled fairly easily and the timbers reassembled elsewhere. They had the valuable privilege of cutting down and selling trees growing on their tenements. Copyholders with only a life tenancy, however, were obliged to keep the property in repair and could only fell trees for timber to carry out repairs.

Provided that the court homage agreed, copyholders could enclose parcels of wasteland adjoining their houses to increase the size of their gardens and orchards, or to erect sheds or carthouses; but they could not take wasteland to build a new house. Rents went up accordingly. Such enclosure was easy as most head tenements were around the edges of pieces of common.

To prevent the dismemberment of the head tenements, inheritance was only allowed to the eldest son and should there be no sons, only to the eldest daughter. Many of the undersetters were sons of head tenants.

WASTEHOLD

Cottages were sometimes built as encroachments upon the commons, especially in Weald. If they were permitted by the manor court to remain, they became known as wastehold properties.

THE HEAD TENEMENTS AND OPEN FIELDS

A number of rentals and surveys from the thirteenth century onwards give information about the property holdings. The head tenements were spread about the hamlets thus by the sixteenth century:[9]

Harrow-on-the-Hill 13, Pinner 21, Roxeth 13, Weald 12, Greenhill 5, Alperton 8, Uxendon 4, Wembley 4, Kenton 2, Preston 2 and 17 cotlands in Sudbury.

The tenement normally consisted of a residence standing within its own small hedged fields, with the selions scattered about the open fields of the hamlet in which it was situated. The names of the tenements, like Sweetmans in Pinner, often derived from the surname of an early owner, in that case, John Swetman who was alive in 1337. The tenement names tended to linger on as field names even if the house fell into decay and was demolished. Most of the head tenements were on the edge of common land and had presumably been built originally on land cleared from it. Several men owned more than one head tenement.

All the hamlets except Harrow-on-the-Hill and Sudbury had open fields, generally smaller than those found in neighbouring manors like Ruislip. Weald and Roxeth each had two separate groups of open fields.

36. Sweetmans Hall in West End Lane c.1930.

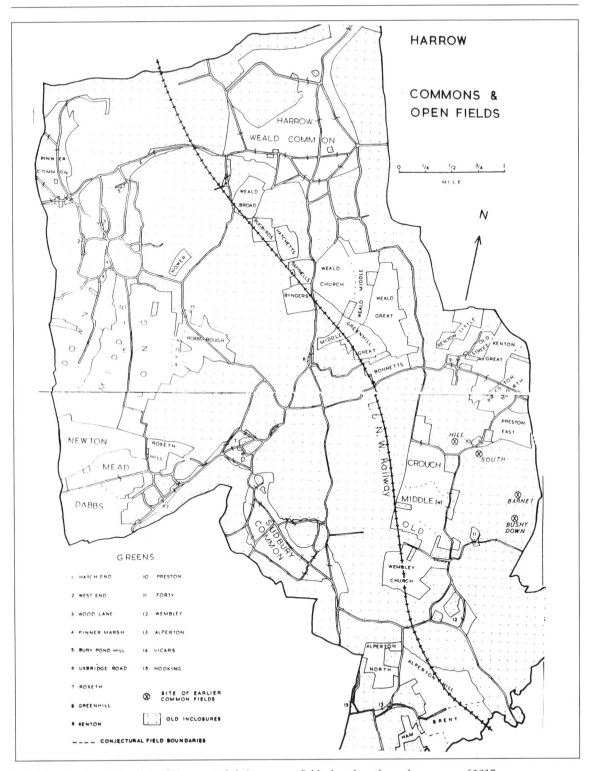

37. *Map showing the hamlets of Harrow and their common fields, based on the enclosure map of 1817.*

HARROW-ON-THE-HILL AND SUDBURY

There were 13 head tenements at Harrow-on-the-Hill in the 1230s, each with a yardland, but the lands soon seem to have been divided into smaller units and there were no open fields there. When a weekly market and annual fair started in Harrow in 1261 on the fields running down the back of West Street to Bessborough Road, the business engendered by them probably encouraged the building of new houses and the development of trades. Harrow-on-the-Hill became more of a town with the settlement centred on High Street, West Street and Hog Lane (later called Crown Street). Sudbury also had no open fields, but extensive common land. Sudbury Common was a large wooded area in medieval times and the cotlanders had their cottages and 5 acre crofts around its edge. Their animals seem to have been mainly sheep which grazed the common, perhaps hastening the clearance of the woodland. The farmland in Sudbury mainly belonged to the demesne centred on Sudbury Court.

ROXETH AND GREENHILL

Roxeth had three fields, Dobbs or Dabbs, Newton (formerly Blackhall) and Mead or Middle Field. The head tenements straggled along Roxeth Green (now Northolt Road). In 1547[10] the head tenements were called Crythes, Cooks, Kings, Kings alias Barbors, Cock Goodwynnes, Hurlockes, Nycholls, Frends and Brettons.

At Greenhill two head tenements, Lampitts and Hawkins, were in the hands of John Greenhill by 1547, one to the south and the other to the east of Greenhill Green[11]. The green was around the junction of the modern Station Road, Sheepcote Road and Bonnersfield Lane. William Greenhill had another called Huttons, which could be the house in the bend of Bonnersfield Lane known in the nineteenth century as the Manor House. The other two head tenements were owned by Henry Finch, one being named Dyaches or Dyetts and the other Finches or Coles. One of those stood on the west side of Greenhill Lane and later became Hill's Farm (latterly called

38. Piepowder House 1791. The Piepowder (probably from the French 'pied poudre', meaning dusty foot) courts that dealt with misdemeanours at fairs, are believed to have been held here. Part of the building can be seen in the alleyway beside 69 West Street.

39. This may be one of the Greenhill family's head tenements at Greenhill, known as Huttons in the sixteenth century. It was later altered and called the Manor House in the nineteenth century.

Fairholme). The five common fields were North, East, West, Greenhill and Bandon Fields, but by the seventeenth century West Field appears to have been enclosed and the other four fields had become just three, Great, Middle and Bonners Fields.

THE WEALD

The Weald, later known as Harrow Weald, running from Greenhill north to the county boundary, took its name from the woodland from which the fields and closes, were cleared. There were two main settlements, one along the edge of the woodland near Hatch End and the other at the 'lower end of Weald', (Boxtree Road, Elms Road, top of Kenton Lane) and open fields to the south in what is modern Wealdstone. The position of the open fields suggests that clearance of the woodland for arable land had begun at the southern, flatter end of Weald, but encroaching on Weald Wood, the hilly, wooded common to the north, went on apace in the sixteenth and seventeenth century, cottages with gardens being erected, usually without licence from the lord of the manor. A map drawn by Benjamin Hare in 1614[12] entitled *Harrowe Weale in Comitatu Middlesexiae*, shows the woodland dipping south of the Uxbridge Road, with an area of open common labelled 'The Green' filling most of the space between the woodland and the houses. Thirty-one cottages or houses with the names of the occupiers are shown along the southern fringe of the green. There were 12 more on the edge of the woodland on the east side of Clamp Hill and nine houses in the middle of the woodland. A brick kiln house with a substantial house nearby belonging to Mr Nelson was also in the woodland beside a track called White Way and there were two houses or cottages near

40. Honeybun Farm, Roxeth, was one of the tenements on the edge of Roxeth Green. It was demolished in the 1920s.

41. *Harrow Weald House Farm survives in Elms Road.   The portion seen here on the left dates from c.1600.   It was on the edge of the woodland at 'the lower end of the Weald'.   It became the bailiff's cottage of the Harrow Weald House estate in the nineteenth century.*

Bentley Corner. Several tracks are shown crossing the wooded common, converging at Bentley Corner. One on the eastern side probably equates with the modern Clamp Hill. Another is fairly close to the modern Brookshill. White Way coming from Hatch End has disappeared, as has a winding track leading from ground belonging to New College, Oxford, on the north-west side

42. The Seven Balls in Kenton Lane was a tenement called Corner Hall in the seventeenth century.

of the wood to a house owned by the college at the corner of Clamp Hill and Uxbridge Road.

Among the 12 head tenements were Astmiss and Causeway Gate, Waldo's Farm, Weeles and Deerings, all between Hatch End and Kenton Lane. Land on the eastern side of the woodland belonged to Bentley (Bentley Priory) which had ceased to have a prior before the end of the fifteenth century. The chapel there had had no priest to say mass for two years according to the court roll for 1512 and after the dissolution of the monasteries had passed into lay hands.

The open fields attached to the 'lower end of Weald' were north-west of the Wealdstone or Lidding Brook, and were called Great, Middle and Church Fields. The last named seems to have been known as Bregges or Bridge Field in the fifteenth century and the change in name is probably due to the fact that the bridge (in Wealdstone High Street) was called Church Bridge, perhaps because it was on the route to St Mary's church. The other settlement had no separate open fields in the sixteenth century, but later some closes belonging to messuages became

43. East End Farm Cottage in Moss Lane, Pinner. Part of the building dates from the fifteenth century. It is perhaps the cottage called Redinges in the sixteenth century.

Broad and Byngers open fields and there were three others by the late eighteenth century, Bugbirds, Hatchetts and Swynells.

The head tenements of Pinner were scattered around the centre of the hamlet at West End, East End, Nower Hill, Pinner Marsh, Bridge Street, Love Lane and Paines Lane, with an isolated one called Gardiners at the top of Potter Street Hill. Three open fields, East or Long Field, Middle Field and Down Field were in the southern area where Rayners Lane and the modern roads off it are today.

KENTON, PRESTON, UXENDON, WEMBLEY AND ALPERTON

All these hamlets had open fields. The two head tenements in Kenton were Wapses and Jacketts, situated near Kenton Green. The open fields, Great, Little and Gore Fields, lay east of the green, to the boundary with Great Stanmore. There were five open fields in Uxendon, Crouch, South, Barnet, Uxendon and Bushey Down Fields. Crouch and South Fields were shared with Preston, which also had North Field and East Field. Alperton had four, Brent, Hill, North and Ham Fields. Wembley's open fields were enclosed early, leaving only 35 acres of open field land by 1547.

CROPS

Wheat and oats were the chief crops grown in the open fields and on the demesne farms of the Archbishop of Canterbury in the thirteenth and fourteenth centuries, with some maslin and peas and beans. Oats became less common in the sixteenth century. Animals could graze on the fallow fields and pigs could forage in the woodland on payment of pannage.

[1] London Metropolitan Archives: Acc 310/4.
[2] LMA: Acc 1052.
[3] Bowlt, Eileen M. *The Goodliest Place in Middlesex* pp 118-9, (1989).
[4] *Ibid.*
[5] LMA: Acc 310/4.
[6] Ibid.
[7] Ibid.
[8] Ibid.
[9] LMA Acc 1052.
[10] Ibid.
[11] Ibid.
[12] LMA: Acc 892.

44. Harrow School 1816.

Harrow School

Since Harrow School was founded in 1572 it has been a mixed blessing for the people of Harrow. The founder, John Lyon, intended it to provide free education for boys of the parish, but not for girls who were specifically excluded. He endowed the school with sufficient lands to maintain buildings and pay a salary to a schoolmaster who must be at least a Master of Arts, and an usher who should be a Bachelor of Arts. Recognising that their income of 40 marks (£26 13s 4d) and 20 marks (£13 6s 8d) per annum respectively, might need supplementing, he allowed them to receive 'foreigners' into the school who would pay fees for teaching and for board and lodging. This enabled the school to increase in size and importance, making the name of Harrow well known far beyond the boundaries of Middlesex. As the school expanded it became a major source of employment and revenue for laundresses, tradesmen and craftsmen and subsequently led to much Victorian building in the streets of Harrow Town.

All this, and certain charitable bequests administered by the school governors, was of benefit to the neighbourhood, but the free scholars, who should have numbered 30, were swamped by the paying pupils and made to feel inferior. Their numbers declined, particularly during the eighteenth century, from 19 in 1730 to seven in 1780. This was partly because of resentment over the social distinctions made at the school between the sons of local tradesmen and farmers and the rest; and also because the classical education then provided was not fitted to such children's needs. The idle and drunken headmaster, the Revd Dr James Cox, absconded in 1746 leaving debts. His successor, Dr Thackeray, headmaster 1746-60, intent upon building up the school's numbers, curried favour with the Whig nobility by granting special privileges to their sons. Also independent tutors who improved the standards of teaching were allowed to charge their own fees, far beyond the means of free scholars. The school might be said by that time to have more or less ceased to function as the Free Grammar School for Harrow boys, as laid down by John Lyon.

JOHN LYON c.1514-92

The Lyon family were landowners in Preston from the fourteenth century. John Lyon (*c*.1514-92), founder of the school, is described as a yeoman in its charter, despite having land in Bedfordshire, Hertfordshire, Essex, Marylebone and Kilburn as well as Harrow, which might suggest a higher social status. He inherited two half-hides, Alens and Bucberds, from his father in 1534 and he made a house at Preston, later known as Lyon Farm, his chief residence. It no longer exists, having been sold for the lands to be developed in the 1920s and demolished in 1960 by Wembley Borough Council who built John Perrin Place on the site, named after the last family to farm there. John Lyon and his wife Joan appear to have had no surviving children, which may account for him leaving much of his property as an endowment for Harrow School.

CHARTER 1572

The school was founded by royal charter which could only have been obtained from Queen Elizabeth with the help of influential friends, so John Lyon was fortunate in his association with William Gerard of Flambards, whose brother, Sir Gilbert Gerard, was Attorney-General at the time. The wording of the charter is sufficiently ambiguous to make it unclear whether a new school was being founded, or an old one refounded. Dated 19 February 1572, it established the Free Grammar School of John Lyon for the instruction of children and youth in grammar 'for all times hereafter coming'. Two poor scholars were to

45. John Lyon's Farm at Preston in 1955, with the Revd H.W.R. Elsley in the foreground. The school sold the farm for redevelopent in the 1920s and it was demolished by Wembley Council in 1960.

46. 'School Bill' (registration) outside the Old Schools early in the twentieth century. The portion of Old Schools to the right of the steps dates from 1819-20 when C R Cockerell altered and extended them. The house covered in ivy which can be seen between the Old Schools and the chapel is Armstrong House, a boarding house established in the 1760s. It was demolished when the War Memorial Building was erected 1921-26.

be maintained at each of the universities of Cambridge (at Gonville & Caius College) and Oxford (college to be at the discretion of the governors). Various roads near Preston, the Harrow Road and that between Edgware and London were to be kept in repair, to make the approach to the school from London easier. Money for this came from the the increasingly valuable Marylebone and Kilburn lands. A trust was transferred to the Commissioners of the Metropolis Turnpike Roads in the nineteenth century and eventually to Harrow Council. Money is distributed among the authorities bordering the roads which John Lyon ordered to be kept in repair.

The governors of the school were enjoined to provide charitable assistance to the poor of Harrow, by giving the 60 poorest householders 6s 8d a piece each Good Friday. Pinner paupers were excluded from this bounty unless there were insufficient poor in the rest of Harrow. The £20 per year which this amounted to was given to the vicar to distribute in the nineteenth century. Surplus money from the charitable bequests was used to help poor people marry and apprentice poor children to a trade and in the nineteenth century for occasional gifts to Pinner Sunday School and Harrow National School. Some 600 children were bound out apprentice at the governors' expense between 1648 from which date records are extant to 1871 when the school's statutes changed and the system ceased.

47. The Old Schools in 1808. This is the brick building erected in 1615 by Thomas Page of Roxey. It contained a schoolroom, governors' room and master's living room. C R Cockerell extended it 1819-20 and added oriel windows and battlements at the same time.

ENDOWMENT

The school's endowment consisted of two head tenements in Preston, a freehold messuage and land in Alperton, 67 and a half selions in Uxendon and eight tenements in Harrow-on-the-Hill. Fuel for the school was to come from land in Kingsbury. The Harrow and Preston property belonged to John Lyon and his wife during their lifetimes and reverted to the school in 1608 after his widow's death. Only then was a new school building erected, by Mr Thomas Page of Roxey, on the slope below the church. It was completed in 1615. It is an early example of a wholly brick building in this part of Middlesex. Being on steep ground it had a basement with the schoolroom above it and a governors' room and master's living room above that. It still stands as the west wing of the Old Schools. The new wing, designed by C.R. Cockerell, was added 1819-20, when the old wing was embellished with crow-stepped gables and oriel window to match. Before 1615 the boys were probably taught at Flambards.

ORDERS & STATUTES 1591

Many years after the foundation of the school John Lyon decreed in his orders and statutes of 1591 (sometimes known as his will) that the school should be divided into five forms, with English spoken only in the First Form. There was to be no playtime except on Thursdays if the weather were fine. Boys were to be punished with the rod, but only moderately. Parents had to provide paper, ink, pens, books, candles and bows and arrows. Archery continued to play a part in the life of the school and shooting for the silver arrow was to become a popular competition at the school for about a hundred years until 1772, when Benjamin Heath, headmaster, substituted speech days instead, because large crowds of undesirables had been attracted to watch and gamble upon the outcome of the archery contest.

48. *Harrow boys with cricket bats c.1830. The Headmaster's House can be seen opposite the bottom of Church Hill.*

DEVELOPMENT OF THE SCHOOL AND THREE REBELLIONS

The master or headmaster lived at the schoolhouse (the Old Schools) until about 1650 when William Hide decided to lease a house on the High Street, probably on the site of the present Headmaster's House. This may have been to enable him to take in more fee-paying pupils to augment his income. A letter from a boy's mother written in 1682, when William Horne, formerly of Eton College, was headmaster, shows that there were then 120 pupils, many of whom lived in boarding houses, run by dames who charged £14 a year, while boys who boarded with the master paid £22 a year. Numbers of pupils kept up under the next headmaster, Thomas Brian 1691-1730, but went down disastrously in the time of his successor, Dr Cox of disorderly life. They rose again during the headships of Dr Thackeray and Robert Sumner to more than 230.

When Sumner died in 1771, his assistant master Samuel Parr, having been passed over for the job, opened a rival school at Hill House on Stanmore Hill, taking some 40 pupils with him. The boys had risen in Parr's favour and had attacked one of the governors' coaches, arguing that as fee payers they were independent of the foundation and that their views should have influence. Parr's school was only successful for a few years and Harrow soon regained its numbers, and a Sixth Form was instituted by Benjamin

Heath (1771-85). He thought it worthwhile to increase the size of the Headmaster's House in 1774, even though £800 came out of his own pocket, but a fire damaged it the following year and only then was an insurance policy taken out.

Joseph Drury (1785-1805) was a patron of the arts and helped establish Edmund Kean at Drury Lane. Byron who was a pupil towards the end of Drury's time at Harrow, regarded him as 'the best and worthiest friend I ever possessed' and led another rebellion against the appointment of George Butler (1805-29) as headmaster in 1805. Gunpowder was laid along the rambling corridors of the Headmaster's House and only the Harrovians' sense of tradition saved Dr Butler from being blown up, as the rebels realised that the panelling carved with the names of their fathers would have been destroyed had they prosecuted their plan. Dr Butler enlarged the house, adding a wing to accommodate more boys, 120 eventually, and added a stone facade to the timber-framed and lath and plaster building.

The people of Harrow chose this time to try to regain the old rights of free scholars against the incomers by entering a plea in Chancery. Among other complaints they said that the wealthy 'foreigners' were a corrupting influence. The judgment delivered in 1810 found in favour of the governors. Butler was something of a reformer and having forbidden the monitors to beat other boys who had committed misdemean-

49. The fire which destroyed the Headmaster's House of Harrow School on Monday, 22 October 1838.

ours with undue severity, found himself faced with another rebellion in 1808. The boys barricaded themselves in the Fourth Form Room and blocked the London Road. The ringleaders were expelled and blanket tossing was forbidden and the evils of fagging tempered, but the free scholars or foundationers continued to suffer humiliation. Anthony Trollope, whose inadequate father had moved to Harrow specifically to obtain a free education for him, recorded his sufferings there in the 1820s and '30s, in his autobiography.

Dr Christopher Wordsworth, nephew of William Wordsworth, the poet, was headmaster 1836-44. The governors in 1836 thought it desirable 'and as likely to promote the best interests of the school, that the boarders should be removed, and in future prohibited in the Headmaster's house' and the maths master, Mr Colenso, offered to build a new house alongside and take over their care. A central heating system was installed and the overheating of its flues was blamed for a disastrous fire breaking out there between six and seven o'clock on the evening of Monday 22 October 1838[1]. The parish fire engine and a small engine kept in Dr Wordsworth's yard proving inadequate, a message was sent to the London Fire Engine Establishment at Baker Street 11 miles away. It took seven minutes to

50. Druries. The present house was designed by C F Hayward and built in 1865. It is decorated with multicoloured bricks and elaborate motifs carved in the stone around the windows.

51. *The first school chapel was built in 1839 greatly to the chagrin of the vicar of St Mary's, the Revd J W Cunningham. This drawing shows C R Cockerell's first design, which was slightly modified in the actual building.*

52. *A view taken about 1900 showing Dr Vaughan's school chapel, designed by Sir George Gilbert Scott and built between 1854-56. Beyond can be seen the Speech Room which was built in 1874 to commemorate the school's tercentenary in 1872.*

harness the four horses to the engine and the equipage was drawn to Harrow in 35 minutes, arriving shortly after half past eight. The glow in the sky had attracted the attention of Mr Charles Blackwell of Harrow Weald, who had immediately sent to Bentley Priory for the Marquess of Abercorn's engine, which had arrived about eight o'clock. Later another engine came from Brentford. Unfortunately the pipes were too short to reach the ponds at the Grove and the Park as well, so a bucket chain brought water from the Park, and one of the pipes laid to the Grove was found to have been cut! The fire was not brought under control until the next morning and smouldered on in the cellars until the end of the week. Looters and ruffians from as far away as London followed the engines to Harrow and Special Constables were hastily sworn in to try and preserve order, to little avail.

The new boarding house, the Headmaster's House and the home of the surgeon, Mr Bowen, were gutted and a saddler's and baker's premises were damaged. Fortunately there was no loss of life, although a boy who was lying dangerously ill had to be carried out of the house in a blanket. Strangely, the house had only been newly insured a few days before. Henry Drury, son of the former headmaster, watched the fire from Druries House opposite. 'It was a magnificent sight in Mr Colenso's long passage to see hall, playroom, study, and every window in the yard sending out volumes of flame' he wrote in a letter to his son at Caius College. From the townspeople's point of view the fire resulted in the acquisition of a superior fire engine, the repair of the old one and the cleaning of the pond in Byron Hill Road to increase the water supply. An engine house was built in Hog Lane (now

53. *The Vaughan Library of 1863, which was built after Dr Vaughan had gone to Doncaster, is another of George Gilbert Scott's designs, where he uses patterned tiles to decorative effect.*

Crown Street). Dr Wordsworth removed to a cottage in Roxeth Hill until a new house was erected. The governors had to borrow money as the school had been underinsured. Mr Colenso at first agreed to rebuild the boarding house, but took over Harrow Park instead when the master there, Mr Phelps, left Harrow.

Dr Wordsworth's main contribution to Harrow School was the building of a chapel in 1839, large enough to accommodate all the boys, where he could influence them by his sermons. Sir Robert Peel who had been at Harrow, was offended by Wordworth's high-church views and sent his younger sons to Eton. Numbers dropped during this period to only 70, partly because of the loss of the boarding accommodation in the fire. Discipline seems to have been lax. Boys in their free time continued to throw stones, fight each other and hunt hares on foot. From 1834-7

beagles known as *Canes Hergenses* were kept in a cottage pigsty at Roxeth (later at Greenhill) by boys who hunted hares on foot three days a

54. *The Foss boarding house was built in Grove Hill in 1859 with diaper patterned brick work and stepped gables. It was designed by E Habershon.*

week, without the knowledge of, or more probably with the connivance of the masters. They slipped down ropes let out of their windows before dawn on Tuesdays, which were whole holidays and often had to wait for daylight to find their first hare. The Thursday and Saturday half holidays were also occupied by hunting.[2]

Dr Wordsworth's successor, Dr Vaughan (1845-59) from Rugby, came imbued with Arnold's principles when only 28 years old. He was allowed to build a boys' wing onto the new Headmaster's House and later added an extra storey as the school's fortunes improved. Numbers having increased to 460, a larger chapel was necessary which was built at his own expense around the former brick one. It was designed by George Gilbert Scott and built by Richard Chapman of Grange Farm, Roxeth between 1854-56. The New Schools were erected in 1855. The residents of Harrow were again concerned about free education or at least a suitable education for their sons and appealed to the governors to found a commercial school for them. This was rejected, but Dr Vaughan established an English Form in an old coach house in Roxborough Road, where Latin would be taught free of charge, but £5 a year

56. The Butler Museum and Museum Schools, designed by Basil Champneys, were completed in 1886 just after Dr Butler had left the school. The open staircase suggests a French chateau.

had to be paid for other subjects and it was understood that pupils could not claim the rights of Lyon scholars (the exhibitions at Oxford and Cambridge), nor mix with the boys at the 'higher' school.

Dr Vaughan after a successful 15 years went away to be vicar of Doncaster and was followed at the school by the Revd Montagu Butler (1860-85), son of George Butler, the former headmaster. He was responsible for two of the important school buildings, the Vaughan Library of 1863

55. The interior of the Speech Room c.1980. William Burges was the architect.

57. *Church Hill in 1928 with a view of the War Memorial Building by Sir Herbert Baker and built between 1921-26. The shops on the left were demolished in 1929 to make a new terrace for the Old Schools.*

and the Speech Room of 1874. The library commemorated his work at Harrow, not his life – he did not die until 1897. The Speech Room marks the three-hundredth anniversary of the school in 1872. Evidence given to the Royal Commission looking into the running of certain schools and colleges in 1864, shows that the headmaster received an annual salary of £50 from the governors, but made up his income to £6,000 net from the profits of his boarding house and capitation fees. He was, however, partially responsible for the repairs of the school buildings. By this time the foundation scholars were culled from the higher social classes, who were being encouraged to take houses in Harrow because of this privilege which was mentioned in property advertisements. There were 24 tradesmen's sons in the English Form. The curriculum in the main school included maths and modern languages as compulsory subjects as well as the classics. The commissioners decided that the class distinctions at Harrow School should be abolished, by stopping the free places and not reserving the university exhibitions for boys born in Harrow! The school would become open to the public at large, in fact a public school. The new statutes took effect from

1868 when the Public Schools' Act became law. In lieu of the foundation places a new school was to be opened for the English Form. It was opened as the Lower School of John Lyon in 1876, a fee-paying school for the middle classes, which was maintained by 'the Keepers and Governors of the possessions, revenues and goods of the Free Grammar School'.

The sciences were introduced into the curriculum during Butler's headship, but their study was not greatly encouraged until the time of the First World War. The next head, Revd J.E.C. Welldon (1885-98) suggested that boys should sit the Civil Service and other public examinations. Shops were cleared from the side of the school yard by Lionel Wood (1910-25), who also built the War Memorial Building on the site of two former school houses, Armstrong and Church Hill.

The school in 1998 had 766 pupils and 11 school houses. It takes pride in having produced seven prime ministers, including Peel, Palmerston and Churchill, and playwrights and poets like Sheridan and Byron.

58. The Headmaster's House on the High Street early in the twentieth century. It was built to replace one damaged by fire in October 1838.

THE SCHOOL ESTATE

As housing estates began to creep over the former fields around the bottom of the hill in the later part of the nineteenth century, the governors endeavoured to surround the school buildings with a 'green belt' of playing fields. By 1911,

59. Harrow School Laundry was built in Alma Road in 1890 to the designs of E S Prior. It provided employment for the people of Roxeth.

through the gifts and bequests of old Harrovians the immediate environment had been secured. Laborde was able to write, 'a solid rampart has now been reared against attack on the London side. The Park, the Football fields and the Northwick estate keep us safe there. The securing of the Grove Fields completes the assurance that old Harrovians returning to Harrow, even after many years, will henceforward find it as they remember it.'[3] He considered that changes towards Roxeth and Wealdstone were of no account as they were out of sight. In more recent years the school itself has caused unease to the inhabitants of the hill by building the school theatre on open land at the back of West Street.

Sources:
VCH Middlesex Vols I and IV
Druett W W: *Harrow Through the Ages* (1935).

[1] May, Trevor F: 'The destruction by fire of the Headmaster's House', *London and Middlesex Historian* No. 1 (1965).
[2] Harrow Central Reference Library: *The Harrovian*.
[3] Laborde, *Harrow School Yesterday and Today* (1948).

Woodlands and Commons

WEALD COMMON

Weald Common was the area of wooded common land stretching from the houses of the Lower End of Weald south of the Uxbridge Road, to Bushey Heath in the extreme north-east corner of the parish, about 700 acres in size. The whole of it belonged to the lord of the manor, but his tenants had common rights over it. It was known as Weald Wood until the seventeenth century, but had become Weald Common by 1666.[1] The Terrier (land survey) of Harrow,[2] made in 1547 shortly after Sir Edward North took over the manor, describes 'Welde Wood' as 420 acres within the larger common, 'lying open and common and thynsett with Beche and hardburgh'. (Hardburgh almost certainly means hornbeam. Harber, found in dictionaries of archaic words, has that meaning). It sounds as if the wood, although unenclosed, was being coppiced or pollarded, as the document continues 'whereof there is in waste ground 140 acres and 80 acres of one hundred years growth valued at 53s 4d the acre, 80 acres growing by parcels of 80 years growth valued at 40s the acre and 120 acres residue of 50 and 60 years growth valued at 20s the acre   ...The said wood lies 10 miles from London and 7 miles from Braynesford (Brentford) where the Thames is currant to London and there may be made in every acre...30 loads of talwood [poles cut to a standard length of 4 feet for fuel] and 20 ... of coles [charcoal] ...' The suggestion implied is that transport to the London market was easy and that talwood and charcoal used for domestic fuel and industry in Tudor London, would make a good profit.

Part of the common, 45 acres, still exists bounded on the south and east by Old Redding and Common Road. It is now known as Harrow Weald Common and was preserved by an Act of Parliament passed in 1899, at the instigation of W.S. Gilbert (of Gilbert & Sullivan fame) who was living at the time at the house called Grimsdyke (now a country club hotel) which had been built on a piece of former common in 1870-2. Part of the common was set aside as gravel pits at the time of the Harrow Enclosure in 1817 and the diggings which continued until

60. *Weald Common.*

the 1899 Act are evident today. The area is now overgrown and has a good deal of oak of more than a hundred years' growth, widespread beech, birch, a little hornbeam and some gorse (furze). It is in the care of the Borough of Harrow. There is no sign today of coppicing.

However, the name of Copse or Weald Coppice Farm on the south side of Old Redding, which was cleared from the wooded common by the lord of the manor during the later part of the seventeenth century, seems to indicate that these lost portions of the wood were the sections which had been managed to produce timber and fuel. One parcel, about five acres in size, of the old woodland remains south of Old Redding and west of the fields of Copse Farm. On the 1864 OS six-inch map it is marked Weald Wood and is now open to the public. Within it can be seen possible remains of coppiced oak and coppiced hornbeam as well as holly and silver birch. The boundary bank which surrounds it probably dates from the seventeenth century when the fields of Copse Farm were gradually being cleared and would have preserved the coppice within from the depredations of grazing animals. There is evidence here, too, of gravel digging, probably from the sixteenth century before the wood was enclosed.

61. *Grimsdyke House was built for the painter, Frederick Goodall in 1872, to designs by R. Norman Shaw. W. S. Gilbert lived here from 1890 until his death in 1911 and he ensured that Harrow Weald Common should be preserved by Act of Parliament.*

SUDBURY COMMON

Another area of woodland, about 300 acres, covered Sudbury Common, spreading on either side of London Road, Sudbury Hill and Harrow Road from Roxeth Hill to beyond Sudbury Station. No trace of this woodland remains today.

COMMON RIGHTS

The commons were owned by the lord of the manor, but tenants had certain rights, which were not clearly defined. During the seventeenth century the lords of the manor, Lord North and later George Pitt sought to establish what these were. An inquiry apparently held at the manor court 15 April 1618[3] showed that some of the people of Weald had encroached upon the common to build cottages without the lord's licence or leave of the tenants, while others had added 'parcels of increase' taken in from the lord's waste to existing houses. Benjamin Hare's 1614 map of Harrowe Weale clearly shows about a dozen such cottages.[4] Some of these tenants' names appear on the Hare map. Sometimes of late years fines had been taken by constraint for

62. *Weald Wood, the five acres on the south side of Old Redding which are open to the public. This picture, taken in September 1999, shows relict coppiced oak and hornbeam.*

the increases, but no fines had ever been paid otherwise.[5]   Nine men and one woman, who were presented by the homage for building cottages, were ordered to lay open the encroachments (take down the fences, but not demolish the cottages) by Michaelmas on pain of 40 shillings should they default.[6]   Tenants could put up cart houses on the waste provided they did not fence them round.[7]

Such cottages were sometimes granted to the tenant retrospectively and known as wastehold. 'One cottage situate in Weald Wood now in possession of Richard Allen parcel of the lord's waste' was granted to Richard and his wife, Lydia in October 1634, on condition that 'if they shall not pay yearly 2 shillings or if they shall receive any inmate into the messuage or do spoil the lord's wood, then this grant be null and void'.[8]

At the 1618 manor court it was stated that copyholders of inheritance had always been permitted to fell timber growing on their own land and dispose of it and could pull down any messuage or other building on their copyhold land.[9]   They, along with freeholders, were also allowed to dig and take sand, loam and gravel, wherever convenient in the lord's waste for the necessary use of repairing or re-edifying their *ancient* messuages and attached buildings, but not for 'new erected cottages which have been erected within memory.'[10]   It was evident that much digging had been taking place for other purposes such as making bricks.   William Wellshin of Wealdstone, (an early use of this place-name), was a culprit at Weald and William and Thomas Butt had done the same thing on the waste at Roxeth.[11]   In 1629 after Robert Page had been presented at court for digging loam and sand and Hugh Bird for digging loam in an inconvenient place, the homage desired the lord to appoint one or more officers to dig sand, loam or gravel, so that the tenants could buy it at the rate of 2d a load if it were to repair an ancient messuage, or 4d a load if it were for a cottage, plus a reasonable salary to the man who did the digging.[12]

A question had arisen about the lord's right to exploit rabbit warrens, but the homage in 1618 denied any knowledge of such a thing.[13]   They also claimed to know of no spoiling of the lord's wood.   Men had been fined for lopping or cutting down trees.   But in 1631 Richard Ford, Thomas Ellis and three others had to pay 5 shillings each for cutting down, carrying away and spoiling

the lord's woods.   On the same occasion Thomas Jackett and John Lane who had cut furzes on the lord's waste and sold them outside the parish were mulcted 2d each and it was ordered that from that time no one should cut and sell furzes outside Harrow on pain of a 5 shilling penalty.[14]   Two years later it was William Hickman of Bushey who was in trouble for cutting holly in Wealdwood and making off with it in his cart.[15]   The ancient custom of the manor allowed tenants to lop any ash or willow trees which they had planted on the waste themselves in front of their gardens or houses as a protection, but seven feet must be left standing for the lord, because the soil which had nurtured the tree was his.[16]

WOODLAND USES

With so much encroachment upon the woodland and with the cotlanders of Sudbury being allowed to graze their sheep on Sudbury Common, one would have expected the wood pasture in both areas to have been overgrazed, leaving open common.   On the contrary, disputes between lord and tenants over Wealdwood claim that it was so overgrown as to be useless for pasture by 1606.[17]   An agreement was reached whereby Lord North would enclose 150 acres, about a quarter, and leave the rest entirely to the tenants, 'to cutt and grub up and to convert to their own uses the wood and bushes thereon growing and so make the said ground more helpful and useful for the keeping and feeding of cattle'.[18]

63. Copse Farm is now reached along Brookshill Drive. It was built on land cleared from the woodland towards the end of the seventeenth century. The seventeenth/ eighteenth-century house has been encased in later brick.

The enclosed 150 acres of woodland was probably coppiced and became known as Weald Wood, a distinction being drawn between the enclosed wood and the common. George Pitt having succeeded Lord North as lord of the manor in 1636, was advised by a Mr Stone, presumably a lawyer, that he had the right to fell timber on the other three parts of the wood, and could enclose a further third of the woodland provided that 12 standels (standard oaks) were left on each acre, in which case the tenants might insist that the earlier coppice should be laid open again.[19] Mr Thomas Heygate, another of Lord North's advisers, was of opinion that it would be best to fell the new coppice and keep it enclosed with the consent of the tenants and not antagonise them by enclosing any more, 'and then you may fell or lopp upon the other 3 parts what trees or timber you please which will raise you a pretty sum of money and quiet your tenants'.[20]

Pitt granted a 43-year lease of Weald Wood to two tanners, William Finch of Watford and Roger Nicholl of Cowley, from 1652.[21] In 1666 the tenants wished to reclaim all the land as common and six men, 'having a contentious spirit',[22] broke down the fences previously erected around the 150-acre coppice. Edward Palmer, first husband of Alice, the granddaughter of George Pitt, to whom the manor had by then descended, entered a complaint in Chancery[23] and all the defendants except one appeared. The lord's rights were upheld at law,[24] although Edward Palmer entered another Bill of Complaint in Chancery against Nicholl for disposing of the timber trees which his lease did not allow.[25]

Maybe following on from this the enclosed woodland was cleared and developed into Weald Coppice Farm. It was a demesne farm, leased out by the lord of the manor. From the late eighteenth century the tenants were members of the Blackwell family who eventually purchased the farm in 1895. A 1767 inventory shows that wheat was grown on 25 acres, peas and beans on 21 acres and the rest of the 152 acres was given over to hay and raising 150 sheep, 123 pigs and 14 cattle. 12 cart horses pulled the ploughs and wagons. In Victorian times more hay was produced for the voracious London market and fewer arable crops were grown.

WARREN[26]

Despite the homage's denial in 1618, Lord North had a rabbit warren on Sudbury Common from 1608 and George Pitt obtained the agreement of the tenants at the manor court to enlarge it and build a hunting lodge (for hunting deer presumably) on the common in 1640. There had been much trouble during the previous few years between Pitt and Sir Gilbert Gerard of Flambards, who, on pretext of protecting the tenants' pasture from the ravages of the rabbits, had pulled down his rival's first timber lodge. In retaliation Pitt had claimed that Gerard's house, The Hermitage, on the edge of Sudbury Common was wastehold and subject to an entry fine on admission which had not been paid. He sent armed men to evict Gerard's tenant from The Hermitage and left the house with broken windows and an orchard and garden trampled by the cattle which had strayed through the open gates from the common. Gerard, who was a Justice of the Peace, then vented his wrath upon Pitt's luckless warrener by gaoling him for playing bowls on Whit Sunday. When the man died in custody Gerard, who must have been a singularly unpleasant individual certainly not suited to his office, sent the widow to the House of Correction, where she was ill treated and miscarried.

BRICKMAKING

Brickmaking is associated with the wooded parts of Harrow because of the clay, sand and chalk underlying those areas, all of which were used in the brickmaking process. It is clear from the documents quoted above in the section on common rights that bricks were being produced in a small way by individuals, both at Weald and at Roxeth during the seventeenth century. Benjamin Hare's map of 1614[27] shows a 'Brick kiln house' in Wealdwood, south of what is now Copse Farm, which was probably the one leased to Thomas Tibbald at least between 1609-20 by the lord of the manor. During the 1630s Sir Gilbert Gerard of Flambards also made bricks, for a dispute arose between him and Mr Pitt over the digging of sand which was not available on his Flambards estate and subsequently the selling of his bricks at 6d the thousand less than those from the manorial kiln.

The best known kiln was situated near Bentley Corner where the listed Kiln House still stands with the Kiln Nurseries occupying the rest of the site. This kiln belonged to the Bodimeade and

64. *Kiln House, home of the Bodimeade and Blackwell families from the seventeenth century to the 1890s. Only the base of the kiln now remains. This painting by Frederick Goodall, for whom Grimsdyke was built, shows a horse enjoying its rural retirement, having done good service at the Crosse & Blackwell factory in Soho.*

Blackwell families from the seventeenth century to the 1890s. A Bodimeade had a kiln in Barnet in 1652 and a John Bodimeade left his son, Matthew, a kiln at Weald in 1671. A Matthew Bodimeade, perhaps the same one, leased a kiln for brick, tile and lime-making from the lord of the manor in 1685. The family also had brick kilns at Harrow-on-the-Hill and Pinner during the eighteenth century. Mary Ann Bodimeade married Charles Blackwell in 1795 and the couple took over an unexpired lease which she had inherited. It ran for 42 years starting in 1768 at £33 10s per annum[28] and included Pinner Wood and chalk pits there. A lease for Copse Farm, was also taken over.[29]

Brickmaking and the occupations associated with it like chalk digging and mining and lime burning were seasonal and employees usually worked as agricultural labourers as well. The employers were similarly affected and had more than one string to their bow. John Bodimeade (Mary Ann's father) was described as brickmaker and farmer on an insurance policy which he took out with the Royal Exchange Assurance Company in the 1780s.[30] Some seventy years later Mary Ann and Charles Blackwell's eldest son, also Charles, appears as a farmer, brickmaker and tilemaker among the traders in Thomas

Smith's *Handbook for the use of Visitors to Harrow-on-the-Hill* published in 1850. In both cases the farm was Copse Farm.

CHALK PITS AND MINES

The earliest known chalk pit in Pinner was at Waxwell where the chalk came within 10 feet of the surface. In 1647 George Pitt licensed Henry Byrde, John Hearne, Henry Streate and Richard Woods 'to digge & cast upp chalke in his wast ground & Common in Pynnor...in a certeyne place there called Waxwell for the benefitt of themselves, their families & the Common wealth'.[31] They were bound in the sum of £50 to pay him sixpence for every cartload dug. The pit was probably on the west side of Waxwell Lane where the Dell is now with its many tell-tale hollows, but the workings which probably continued far beyond the seventeenth century extended over to the west side of the lane as well. The Pinner Wood chalk pits, leased by the Blackwells, were north of the Uxbridge Road at the Dingles. About the beginning of the nineteenth century mine shafts had been sunk and galleries created on the pillar and stall principle, where areas of chalk are cleared out, leaving blocks or pillars at regular intervals to support

65. This picture shows The City on Old Redding in the 1930s.

the weight above. The earliest mine, which is cruder in style than the others, is thought to date from *c*.1800. Charles Blackwell had two other mines there, one entered through a shaft which has not been found and which may have been cut off by roof falls, as a second shaft was sunk in 1840. A third mine was opened in 1850 and working continued possibly until 1887. Lime kilns at the Dingles provided lime for the brickfield at Harrow Weald and another lime kiln owned by the Blackwells at Bushey Arches supplied the same commodity for another brickfield of theirs at Bushey.[32]

THE KILN

The clay for the bricks at Harrow Weald was dug from the fields opposite The Hare between Brookshill and Clamp Hill, the latter name meaning a stack of bricks layered ready for firing. Other earthenware products such as field drains, pipes, chimney pots and tiles were made at the kiln. The Blackwells lived at Kiln House which dates from the seventeenth century, but was refronted in 1783 and altered internally. In 2000 the base of an updraft bottle kiln still exists on a platform of brick, 60 yards south of the house. It would have stood 40 feet high and was loaded through an aperture on the north-east side and

probably dates from the nineteenth century. A drying shed of eighteenth century date still stands on the east of the house and there are the footings of another alongside. Other buildings were once attached to the kitchen garden wall.

THE CITY

The kiln was obviously successful and led Charles Blackwell to build a group of cottages for his workpeople west of it on the road now known as Old Redding. Two small enclosures on the common there, with three or four cottages on them, were already in his possession at the beginning of the nineteenth century. (Apart from another cottage and garden at the south-western edge of the common south of what is now Boxtree Lane, these were the only properties that he owned as opposed to holding by lease.[33]) By 1831 there were 14 overcrowded cottages inhabited by 120 people, many of whom worked for him and the group was known as The City. The name appears on the 1864 25-inch Ordnance Survey Map. The Hare was already licensed by 1706 but lay on the edge of Weald Common on the east side of Clamp Hill. It had moved to its present location by 1810. The Case is Altered opposite The City was a cottage which belonged to Joseph Ward at the time of the

66. *The Hare was licensed early in the eighteenth century and belonged to Clutterbuck's Brewery, Stanmore, in the nineteenth century. It had moved from the top of Clamp Hill to the building seen here by 1810.*

Harrow enclosure (1803-17) and later became a beerhouse, when it was known jocularly as the Cathedral of The City.

The insanitary and inadequate cottages at The City became an embarrassment to later Blackwells and the oldest ones were replaced in the 1920s by S.J. Blackwell, and R.A. Blackwell handed over the whole group to the Hendon Rural District Council in 1932.[34] Harrow Council succeeded to them and left them empty as the preferential tenants died or moved away. The only traces of their existence today are some of the fruit trees from their gardens and the pump on Old Redding which once supplied them with water.

KILN HOUSE AND COPSE FARM

The Blackwells' eldest son, Charles, who never married, stayed on at Kiln House after his father's death in 1849 and his mother's in 1862. He

67. *The Case is Altered was a cottage which became a beerhouse and was sometimes known jocularly as the Cathedral of The City. The name may derive from the Spanish Casa del Saltar (dancing house) or Casa alta (high house), which may have been known to local men who had served as soldiers in the Peninsular War.*

68. Bridle Cottages. These cottages housed the laundry of the Blackwells' estate.

lived with his sister, Harriet and managed the kiln and Copse Farm until he died himself in 1882. The Blackwells' connection with the kiln ceased about 1895, but according to local reminiscences brickmaking in Clamp Hill carried on until about 1930.[35]

It was during the second Charles Blackwell's time that much building of decorative farmworkers' cottages and other estate buildings went on around Copse Farm. A laundry and several semi-detached pairs still stand in the lane leading from Brookshill to the farm, form-

69. The Dairy Cottage at Copse Farm is a pretty building of the late nineteenth century.

ing a pleasant rural backwater with splendid views across fields towards London. Copse Farm was conveyed to Express Dairies in the 1930s and has been Suzanne's Riding School for many years.

One of Charles' and Mary Ann's younger sons, Thomas, really made the family name. He was apprenticed to Messrs West & Wyatt, oilmen, in King Street, Soho, in 1819, where he met another apprentice, Edmund Crosse. When Mr Wyatt retired in 1829 the young men, by that time out of their apprenticeships, took over the business and Crosse & Blackwell came into being. His descendants lived at Kiln House until the 1930s. The owners of The Kiln Nursery live there in the year 2000.

COLLIERS

Colliers were charcoal burners and they were sufficiently numerous and important in the local economy to have had a part of the present Uxbridge Road named after them. Their work also took place in the woodlands. The 1547 terrier quoted at the beginning of this chapter shows that the trade was flourishing at that time and there are some earlier references from the thirteenth and fourteenth centuries. Perhaps the trade dwindled because seacoal found its way from London to Harrow at a fairly early date.

1. LMA: Acc 76/1022.
2. LMA: Acc 1052.
3. LMA: Acc 76/1009b.
4. LMA: Acc 892.
5. LMA: Acc 76/1009b.
6. *Ibid.*
7. *Ibid.*
8. LMA: Acc 76/2019.
9. LMA: Acc 76/1009b.
10. *Ibid.*
11. *Ibid.*
12. LMA: Acc 76/1013.
13. LMA: Acc 76/1009b.
14. LMA: Acc 76/1013.
15. *Ibid.*
16. *Ibid.*
17. LMA: Acc 76/1022.
18. *Ibid.*
19. LMA: Acc 76/2195.
20. *Ibid.*
21. LMA: Acc 76/1022.
22. *Ibid.*
23. *Ibid.*
24. LMA: Acc 76/1023.
25. LMA Acc 76/1025.
26. *VCH Middlesex*, Vol IV, p227.
27. LMA: 892.
28. LMA Acc 76/2200.
29. *Ibid.*
30. Guildhall MS: 11936/302/462432.
31. Personal possession: Photocopy of agreement dated 16 Feb Charles I, 23 (1648).
32. Druett WW: *The Stanmores and Harrow Weald through the ages,* 1938.
33. Harrow Central Reference Library: Harrow Enclosure Map.
34. Druett: *op. cit.*
35. Harrow Central Reference Library: House Files.

Changing Times

ENCLOSURE OF THE COMMONS AND COMMON FIELDS

Harrow changed from a medieval to a modern landscape at the beginning of the nineteenth century when the commons and common fields were enclosed. As we have seen in earlier chapters there had been encroachment upon the commons for several hundred years and a large part of Weald Common had been enclosed by the end of the seventeenth century. Consolidation of selions in the open fields had led to some of them, for example the Greenhill common fields, being in the hands of only three or four people and there had been much enclosure by the Pages in Wembley and Alperton. Nevertheless at the end of the eighteenth century some 1500 acres of common land (sometimes called the waste) and greens remained open and available for grazing, digging of gravel, loam and sand and the cutting of fuel. There were still about 3400 acres of common fields, the largest amount being in Pinner and Roxeth. Where land was enclosed, there was a shift from arable to the production of hay during the eighteenth century, 46% of the farming land in Harrow being meadow in 1764 and 65% by 1797.[1] Hay, the petrol of the time, was a profitable crop so close to the London market.

ARGUMENTS IN FAVOUR OF ENCLOSURE

The method of agriculture employed in the common fields was under attack from agrarian improvers during the second half of the eighteenth century. The practice of rotating crops (wheat, peas or beans) including a fallow year, meant that roughly one third of the arable land was unproductive. Experiments with new crops like clover, which smothered weeds cleansed the land and made a fallow year unnecessary, were difficult to conduct in fields where every man must work in union with his neighbour. Ploughing being possible in only one direction and not athwart because of the danger of trespassing on neighbouring lands could not produce a good, sweet tilth and drainage was inadequate for the same reason. Time was lost in moving from one strip of land to another.

Reformers believed that the common fields should be enclosed and the land reallocated in consolidated blocks, which could be fenced to enable individual farmers to experiment with crops and new stock-breeding and rearing methods. The expected result of enclosure was increased productivity and hence higher land values and better rent rolls. The common waste was seen as 'wasted land' unprofitable to the lord of the manor to whom it belonged and of not much use to those with common rights either. This last point was arguable especially in Harrow where the digging of gravel etc was a particularly valuable right for the smaller proprietors who had horses and carts to carry it away.

JOHN MIDDLETON'S *VIEW OF THE AGRICULTURE OF MIDDLESEX*, 1798

The Board of Agriculture, set up in 1793 to popularise the new forms of agriculture, caused three reports to be written on Middlesex. That of John Middleton, a land surveyor of West Barn Farm, Merton and of Lambeth, Surrey, published in 1798,[2] said that Middlesex was a very fertile county farmed by conservative people and therefore under productive. The swing plough was still used in favour of the wheeled variety which was easier to keep straight. Drills were not to be seen at all and threshing machines were only just coming into use. Oxen were still the draught animals and used for ploughing. Horses were bought at fairs as they were not bred in the county.

The commons of the county he found were stocked with 'wretched, half-starved animals' whose standard would be improved if the land were drained and limed and fenced to provide better pasture. As for those who used the commons, he believed that few could afford a cow and that those who could were only able to feed it on the commons for three months out of the twelve. Rather than being a loss to the poor, the enclosure of the commons would provide work for them, digging ditches, planting hedges, making wooden fences to protect newly-planted quickset (hawthorn) and making new roads and footpaths. In support of his view he quoted a report from Somerset that '... enclosures have ameliorated their [the poor's] condition, exciting a spirit of activity and industry whereby habits of sloth have been, by degrees, overcome and supineness and inactivity have been exchanged for vigour and exertion.'[3]

Another objection to enclosure, that the costs of fencing the new closes would be so great as to make the acquisition of a small piece of land uneconomic, he dismissed as being easily overcome by selling such land to larger and wealthier landowners.

The payment of tithes would be extinguished at enclosure and replaced by a corn rent charge. Middleton was especially keen to get rid of tithes which he considered oppressive to farmers, pointing out that it was a tax on land, not paid by well-to-do manufacturers and tended to make agriculturalists reluctant to invest in improvements.

OPPOSITION TO ENCLOSURE IN HARROW

It is clear that enclosure would bring major economic benefits to the major landowners, among whom at the end of the eighteenth century were Lord Northwick (the former Sir John Rushout), George Harley Drummond whose Stanmore Park estate included Kenton Lane Farm in Harrow, the Marquess of Abercorn at Bentley Priory and Christ Church College, Oxford, owners of the rectory. The demesne by this time consisted mainly of enclosed farms. Three were in Sudbury, Sheepcote Farm, Woodcock Hill Farm and Sudbury Court Farm. Copse Farm had been enclosed from the woodland at Weald and Sir John Rushout had acquired a head tenement at Greenhill in 1763. However, the lord of the manor stood to gain a substantial allotment to compensate for his loss of rights in the commons.

Middleton refers to a meeting lately held (1796) to discuss enclosure of the commons. The rector

70. Kenton Lane Farm which was part of George Harley Drummond's Stanmore Park estate.

Affociation for Oppofing the *Harrow* Inclofure Bill.

THE COMMITTEE of this ASSOCIATION having been well informed, that the long meditated Bill for inclofing the Wafte and Common Field Lands of the Parifh of *Harrow*, will certainly be brought forward the enfuing Seffions, think proper to apprize you of the intended Meafure, that you may not be taken off your Guard, or conceive that it is revived on any new Principle, or on Terms in any Refpect adequate to the Commonable Rights you now enjoy. The COMMITTEE ftill remain fenfible of the ferious Evils that would refult from fuch Inclofure; and beg Leave to affure you, that they will continue watchful of the general Interefts of the FREEHOLDERS and COPYHOLDERS.

It having been declared by the Promoters of the Inclofure, " that a public Meeting will be called, before any Bill is prefented to the Houfe of Commons," your Attendance at fuch Meeting, (when Notice thereof fhall be given) is particularly requefted, that you may the better judge for yourfelf, of the Difadvantage which muft neceffarily attend fuch an Inclofure, and the Expediency, if not Neceffity, of co-operating with the COMMITTEE in ufing every Exertion to *oppofe the Bill*.

JOSEPH SELLON, CHAIRMAN.

October 27, 1797.

71. Leaflet produced by the Association for Opposing the Harrow Inclosure Bill, October 1797.

(Middleton refers here to Richard Page, lessee of the rectorial tithes) did not attend but sent a letter proposing that 'a particular part of the common containing 300 acres should be allotted to him in one piece, inclosed with a bank, ditch and park paling, and maintained in good repair for ever, at the expense of the other persons who had right of common'.[4] Such an unreasonable demand defeated the intended application.

An *Association for Opposing the Harrow Inclosure Bill* was then formed. Joseph Sellon of Pinnerwood was its chairman in October 1797 when a leaflet was circulated, assuring the public

72. A view of mid-nineteenth century cottages standing on former common in Middle Road.

that the committee would 'continue watchful of the general Interests of the FREEHOLDERS and COPYHOLDERS'.[5] John Baker Sellon of Pinner Hill House was also a leader of this movement.

There was a second attempt at enclosure in 1802, with Richard Page as promoter. All the 271 proprietors of land should have been consulted about the bill to be put through parliament, but only a select few were summoned to a meeting at the Baptist's Head Coffee House in Chancery Lane so that the proposals which should form the basis of the bill could be 'chalked out'.[6] In fact this small group set the composition for tithes, ordered a bill to be prepared, nominated two commissioners and appointed Messrs Neild and Fladgate of Norfolk Street as solicitors. They then invited all the proprietors to attend a meeting at the King's Head, Harrow, on 17 March 1802 'to appoint a commissioner and other matters'.[7] Three commissioners were normally appointed to represent the interests of the lord of the manor, the rector and the proprietors respectively.

The King's Head meeting was crowded, but those who rose to debate the question of tithe composition (the most burning issue) and other

matters, were rudely told by the chairman, Richard Page, that the meeting had merely been called to appoint a third commissioner and that the bill for enclosure would proceed 'whether the proprietors at large approved the measure or not, having sufficient weight of property on their side to overcome all opposition'.[8] The chairman finding himself in conflict with the body of the meeting withdrew and Mr Sellon took the chair and a motion was passed against enclosure. Nonetheless a bill was presented in parliament and having passed two readings was to have gone to committee. At this stage Mr Byng, MP for Middlesex presented a petition[9] against the bill signed by 100 people and obtained leave to be heard in committee. After postponements the bill, as it was late in the session, was abandoned.[10] Joseph Sellon was soon off again in another pamphlet[11] scorning 'all unmanly Triumph upon this Occasion' and promising 'FIRMNESS and VIGILANCE'. He even, towards the end of the document, mentioned the poor – '.. why should they be deprived of those Advantages from the Commons which they have *immemorially* enjoyed ...'

Both sides had to start again and on 6 October 1802 Mr Page on behalf of those in favour of enclosure met Mr Joseph Sellon and Mr Hill who appeared on behalf of the opposition at the Abercorn Arms, Stanmore. Mr Serjeant Sellon (John Baker Sellon was a serjeant-at-law), the solicitor, Mr Fladgate, and the vicar and curate of Harrow were also present. Mr Sellon put forward six proposals, the most important of which concerned the percentage of arable, meadow and waste which should be given in exchange for the extinguishing of tithes. Mr Page refused to negotiate. However, by March 1803, Joseph Sellon was able to announce 'the glad tidings of PEACE and RECONCILIATION'.[12] The two Sellons and Mr Fladgate were to revise the bill without prejudicing the general principles or the interests of the lord of the manor and the lessee of the tithes. Fourteen more years passed while claims for land, exchanges and sales were negotiated, before the Award was published in 1817. Two of the commissioners, Richard Davis of Lewknor and John Trumper of Harefield, had died in 1814 and been replaced by Edward Kelsey of Bury Street, St James's and George Trumper of Harefield. The lord of the manor's commissioner was Jonathan Gibbons of Uppingham, Rutland.

THE ENCLOSURE AWARD and PLAN[13]
Roads

Edward Kelsey and William Rutt surveyed the parish and found that 4750 acres should be allotted and enclosed including footpaths and roads across the new enclosures. The two turnpike roads, Harrow to London and Harrow to Watford, were to be 60 feet wide. These and many other lanes and paths already existed, but had meandered across the commons as dictated by the condition of the ground at different seasons. Henceforth they would be confined between ditches on either side. Lesser roads such as those to Uxbridge, Pinner, Wembley Green and Elstree were set at 40 feet width. Some private roads over Weald Common and elsewhere were to be 30 feet and the footways were mainly three feet wide. Gravel and sandpits were set aside on Weald Common for obtaining materials for mending roads. Harrow School was allowed nearly eight acres of Roxeth Common for a playground, now the school playing fields along Bessborough Road. About 75 people purchased parcels of the former commons, often

73. *The Lower School of John Lyon was built on former common land in 1876.*

that bordering their other land. The money helped defray the costs of enclosure (expenses of commissioners, surveyors and solicitors).

Manorial and Tithe Allotments

Lord Northwick received 71 acres of Weald and Sudbury Commons in compensation for his loss of mineral rights on the waste. The tithe settlement which had been such a bone of contention between the friends and opposers of enclosure, was settled by Christ Church and the vicar of Harrow receiving one ninth of the waste, one fifth of the arable and one ninth of the meadow and corn rents were to be calculated to make up for any shortfall. Christ Church received usefully large but compact blocks of the former open fields of Weald, Greenhill, Preston, Alperton and Pinner and some smaller pieces of common, near Boxtree Road for example. The vicar's lands

74. *The Red House in Middle Road, by E. S. Prior for his brother John T. Prior, whose monogram appears with the date 1885 in the gable, is now part of John Lyon School.*

came in smaller blocks, with a large stretch of Weald Common leading down from Copse Farm to the Uxbridge Road and a slice of the Kenton and Preston open fields and a more modest bite out of Roxeth's.

Apart from the major landowners like Lord Northwick with his 1258 acres and George Harley Drummond with 1172 acres and a few others, the distribution of land after enclosure was as follows:

49 with less than one acre
69 with between 1 and 10 acres
63 with between 11 and 50 acres
18 with between 51 and 100 acres
18 with between 101 and 250 acres
 9 with between 251 and 400 acres.

RESULTS OF ENCLOSURE
New Farms

Many of the small enclosures were along Lower Road, Roxeth Hill, and on Sudbury Common whose 235 acres had been divided into 92 plots, 60 of which were less than an acre in size. These lent themselves to the building of cottages and other small houses. Larger allotments at Harrow Weald tended to be developed as country houses with attendant service cottages for staff near them. Building began in a small way soon after the award was published, and continued through-

76. Down's Farm in Cannon Lane, Pinner was built on newly enclosed land towards the middle of the nineteenth century.

out Victoria's reign and has never ceased.

Some new farmhouses were built. Tithe Farm in Roxeth, Down's Farm in Pinner and Greenhill Tithe Farm. Very little is known of this latter farm except that it was a cottage, barn and out-buildings with 79 acres, covering the area of Wealdstone north of Canning Road and east of Byron Road, which was part of Christ Church's tithe enclosure. It was leased by Christ Church to Henry Young for 21 years in 1859 and part was sublet to a cattle dealer called Henry John Smith in 1874.[14] Farming continued the trend started in the eighteenth century, turning from the production of crops to hay and dairying, which became important in Roxeth and on the

75. Down's Farm.

77. Roxeth School was built in 1851 in memory of Lord Shaftesbury's son. The earlier National School may have been on the same site. The land was former common.

demesne farms. Sheepcote and Greenhill increased as new building brought in an urban population.

All the farms were hit by the agricultural depression of the late 1820s and the 1830s. Lord Northwick, who was accused by the tenants of not repairing his farms, was obliged to lower the rents, but still the farmers could not afford to pay them. Thomas S. Grimwade took over the lease of Sheepcote Farm about 1840 from Henry Longman who had been in difficulties. He wrote to Lord Northwick in 1856 saying that he 'had lost on this farm upwards of £4000 in sixteen years. Indeed it was this loss that sent my poor wife to a premature grave and deprived a young family of maternal care'.[15] He had started experimenting with dried milk in the 1840s and must have recovered as The Desiccated Milk Company was floated in 1857.

The Landscape

A comparison between the Enclosure Map of 1817 and the six-inch Ordnance Survey Map 1868 reveals the change in the landscape, with all the former common fields, having been divided into smaller fields, albeit on the whole larger on average than the old enclosures.

78. The Lodge to Sheepcote Farm c.1910. Thomas Grimwade of Sheepcote Farm supplied desiccated milk to troops in the Crimea. Florence Nightingale endorsed the product in March 1856.

79. *Middle Road and Roxeth Hill were formally laid out, across common land, at the time of the enclosures. The houses in Middle Road and the Half Moon in Roxeth Hill, photographed c.1890, were built on new enclosures in the middle of the nineteenth century.*

80. Tithe Farm, Roxeth, was built following the enclosures on land allocated to Christ Church, Oxford, the Rectors of Harrow. It survived until the 1950s and Tithe Farm Avenue lies to the west of the old farmhouse. Rowe Walk, named in 1956 after the last farmer, is on the actual site. The barn was replaced by the Tithe Farm public house in 1935.

THE POOR

The effect of enclosure upon the poor is much more difficult to ascertain. The effect of the Napoleonic Wars, being prosecuted during almost the whole of the long drawn out enclosure proceedings in Harrow, confuse the picture. Spending on the poor increased, but the rise cannot be wholly attributed to enclosure. The agricultural labourers suffered especially during the agricultural depression and some of the poor might have fared better had there still been the commons, where fuel could be had and greens in the various hamlets, on which geese could have been grazed. Perhaps the fact that 105 people crowded into the workhouse in March 1819 tells its own story.

1   *Victoria County History, Middlesex*, Vol IV.
2   Middleton, J: *View of the Agriculture of Middlesex* (1798).
3   *Ibid*: 2nd edition (1807), p124.
4   *Ibid*: p 60-1.
5   Harrow Central Reference Library: Enclosure Papers A.
6   LMA: Acc 76/2223.
7   Harrow Central Reference Library: Enclosure Papers B.
8   *Ibid*.
9   LMA: Acc 76/2218.
10   LMA: Acc 76/2217.
11   Harrow Central Reference Library: Enclosure Papers D
12   *Ibid*: Enclosure Papers E.
13   Harrow Central Reference Library: Enclosure Award and Plan.
14   Stanmore & Harrow Local History Society *Newsletter 1992*.
15   Harrow Central Reference Library: Harrow Farms File.

81. *Vestry meetings sometimes repaired to the Anchor or Crown and Anchor, handily situated at the bottom of Church Hill. It is seen on the right of this picture which was drawn shortly after the fire at the Headmaster's House in October 1838. The inn was replaced by shops in the mid-nineteenth century, which were swept away in their turn to make way for the new terrace below the Old Schools in 1929.*

Thrown on the Parish

THE VESTRY

The instrument of local government from the beginning of the seventeenth century was the vestry, a group of leading parishioners – mainly gentry, tradesmen and farmers – meeting in the vestry room of the parish church. In earlier times the vestry had dealt with ecclesiastical matters, but the 1601 Poor Law greatly increased its sphere of influence by placing the burden of the care of the poor upon the parish, which meant appointing overseers of the poor and levying and disbursing a poor rate. The supervision of other work formerly the responsibility of the manor courts, such as the maintenance of highways, also transferred to the vestry. The constable eventually became a parish officer, receiving his expenses from the overseers, although he was appointed at the manor court and had to be sworn before justices of the peace. The vestry minute books for Harrow, which are extant from 1704 show that the meetings were usually held in inns during the eighteenth century – The Plough, The Castle, The Anchor, The King's Head and The Paytable – and then in the chancel of the church and in the vestry only from 1849. In 1822 the vestry was forbidden to eat and drink at parish expense, so maybe the move to the chancel was instigated by the vicar to preserve the weaker brethren from temptation!

The overseers of the poor's accounts survive from 1684 and show that seven to ten men usually attended vestry meetings held six to eight times a year in the seventeenth century. On 15 December 1684 they were John Page, John Harris, Samuel Greenhill, John Osmond, Thomas Finch, Thomas Marde, Richard Street, William Dark, Thomas Page and Henry Finch.[1] The Pages were large landowners in the Wembley area and the Greenhills and Finches were prominent farmers in Roxeth and Greenhill, while John Harris farmed part of Sir Charles Gerard's Flambards estate. In the eighteenth century the numbers attending increased to about twenty and meetings were held more frequently, about once a month. During the agricultural depression of the 1820s and '30s the vestry met almost fortnightly to deal with the general distress.

THE POOR

The administration of the poor law consumed most of the vestry's attention. Labourers earned insufficient to tide them over in times of crisis. They needed assistance during periods of accident and sickness, at seasons when there was little work available and nearly always in old age when they were 'past their labour'. Widows and orphaned children only rarely managed without support and there were always tradesmen who fell upon hard times. The 1601 Act obliged the parish to provide the aged and infirm with a place of asylum, give work to the able-bodied poor and apprentice poor children to a trade. The money came from a rate levied upon all types of property, administered by overseers of the poor working within the framework of the vestry. There were three overseers for the parish of Harrow, one for Harrow Town, Sudbury and Roxeth, one for Harrow Weald and Greenhill and another for Wembley, Alperton, Kenton and Preston.

The amount paid out increased noticeably in the later 1690s, varying from £151 1s in 1689 to £346 9s 2d in 1697, a time of general famine and hardship throughout the country. The number of rates levied each year varied to meet the needs of the time. There were five rates in 1740 raising £521, but only one in 1760 bringing in £172. During the economic upheavals of the Napoleonic Wars, which coincided with the struggle for enclosure of the open fields and commons, there were usually five or six rates resulting in sums of £1660 to £2040. The agricultural depression caused such hardship that £3331 was needed in the early 1830s, at a time when the main rate-payers, the farmers, were themselves in trouble.

82. The Castle Inn in Crown Street was rebuilt in 1901. Its predecessor provided a venue for vestry meetings.

83. There was a church house in the churchyard used to house poor widows in the seventeenth and eighteenth century. This is a view of the churchyard about 1860.

PARISH HOUSES

There does not seem to have been a special 'place of asylum' provided in Harrow, but there are several references to parish houses, probably old and decrepit cottages taken over by the parish. A survey of cottages at Weald taken in 1677[2] states that Margaret Edlin and the Widow Field were living in two tenements 'where the parish have placed them pretending they are parish houses ... pay no rent'. Widow Hely had been put in another close by. These three tenements claimed by the parish were valued at £2 5s altogether. There was also a church house in the churchyard used to accommodate widows. Some people like Widow Bond and Goodman Love in 1695, probably remained in their own houses, but had their rents paid for them.[3] This seems to have been common practice in Harrow. 14 people's rents were paid in March 1686.[4] It looks as though the cage house or lock up was not much used for its intended purpose and was invaded by poor squatters. The constable in 1751 was ordered to turn out the people living in it and clean it and 'keep it for the use it was first designed for'.[5]

PENSIONS AND CASUAL ASSISTANCE

In the 1680s the amount discharged on behalf of the poor was heaviest in March and lightest in April and May. The late winter was the period when fresh food supplies were at the lowest, affecting people's diet, making them prone to infection. Most of the disbursements were in the form of pensions varying from 2 shillings to 10 shillings a month each. When Faith Winch was put into the church house in the churchyard in 1707, she was given a flock bed, sheet and blankets and a pension of 4 shillings a month to keep her going.[6] Sometimes such payments were withheld if the overseers believed that they were being imposed upon. William Platt was to receive no further payments in 1754 'til he sends a boy and girl home that he keeps, to the parish they belong to'.[7] Paupers were supposed to receive relief only in their parish of settlement – the place they were born, or where they had worked as a hired servant for a year and a day, been bound apprentice, or served as a parish officer. In November 1724 it was ordered that Widow Butcher 'who takes upon herself the name of Griffin be forthwith removed with all her children to there legal settlements'.[8] This may have split the family if the children had been born in different places.

Other payments were made on behalf of the sick who received medicine and other necessaries, nursing and eventually burial, all at parish expense. In March 1686/7 Widow Freelove and Widow Dancer 'being sick' were given 2 shillings each and 10 shillings went towards 'keeping Edmund Osmond's wife'. She had been on the sick list since the previous November when William Martin's wife was being paid to attend her.[9] Ann Batt had been ill and receiving help and then died and there was a further expense of 17s 6d, in arranging her funeral. At the end of the account, however, the overseers note that they received £2 11s 10d for Ann Batt's goods, which must have been sold after her death.[10] There was a smallpox outbreak in the parish in 1746, when the men at Wembley who had presumably recovered from it, were given half-a-

84. Parishioners probably enjoyed attending vestry meetings at the King's Head.

crown 'to go away' and Widow Wild was allowed an extra shilling because of 'the extraordinary charge she was at with a soldier in the smallpox'.[11]

The parish retained the services of an apothecary and surgeon to care for the poor. Mr Samuel Parr was allowed 10 guineas in 1738 and if patients were ordered to hospital for treatment, the parish agreed to meet the charges.[12] William Hawkes was sent to hospital on 14 May 1746 'to have his eyes couch'd'.

Although bastard children and abandoned families were maintained by the parish, efforts were made by the officials to prosecute irresponsible fathers. Thomas Street was kept in custody in 1746 until he gave a security for the child 'he had begotten on the body of Dorothy Whitehead'.[13]

THE WORKHOUSE

A large body of 22 parishioners turned out for the vestry meeting in May 1724 to discuss building a workhouse in Harrow. Sir John Rushout was thanked for recommending the scheme and it was agreed that the church house, which had simply been a place of asylum for the elderly poor, should be demolished and the materials employed in building the new 'House of Maintenance'. It was built in West Street opposite the Crown Inn. The vestry minutes suggest that members regarded entry to the house as a privilege to be removed from paupers who failed to obey such rules as attending Divine Service. Mrs Holliday, the matron, in January 1754 had orders 'not to lett anybody go out of the house or in unless it is about the parish business and that no person upon no pretence whatever, or of the greatest age, go out without it is to church and that they immediately return after service is over, which if not obeyed she is to keep them out of the house or she be turned out herself''.[14]

The paupers in the house were required to spin mop yarn and the wool was purchased from Mr Jones of Uxbridge in 1733. The female inmates were meant to teach the children how to spin, but some must have rebelled in 1752 and 'denied that they knew how to spin wool and it has since been found out they understand it and have put the parish to the charge of hiring a woman to instruct the children in spinning. It is now ordered that the said women be immediately turned out of the house and not let in again but by order of the justices'.[15]

85. *The 'House of Maintenance' or Workhouse built in West Street in 1724 (35 West Street).*

To begin with the masters of the workhouse were paid a weekly wage, but the care of the poor was farmed out to a master from 1754. He was paid an annual sum out of which he had to maintain the poor in the house and make what profit he could from the sale of their work. In 1795 the master managed on £594, but by 1821 William Mander needed £1400 because of the increasing levels of poverty. A different system had emerged by 1830, whereby the master, Charles Winkley, received a fixed sum of 4s 6d per pauper per week.[16] He was also in charge of Great Stanmore workhouse

The Harrow workhouse, which is now a private residence (35 West Street), could accommodate 60 people, but the numbers fluctuated according to season and economic conditions. In 1747 there were 59 people resident in February, but only 30-33 in the previous autumn when the sowing of winter wheat provided employment. 105 crowded in during March 1819 a couple of years after the loss of the greens and commons because of enclosure.

Outdoor relief continued to be given and a sliding scale of allowances based upon the number of children in a family was in operation from 1795. During the agricultural depression the allowance was reduced and more parish work was found, picking oakum and at the mill or on the roads. Single men were sent to work for local farmers who were obliged to take them on at fixed wages. When the Poor Law Amendment Act became law in 1834 Harrow became part of the Hendon Union and according to law outdoor assistance was supposed to be abolished, but a paid relieving officer visited the various parishes to relieve hard cases as ordered by two justices.

THE HENDON UNION

Adjacent parishes formed Unions to provide workhouse accommodation and the relief of the poor. Harrow was joined by Great and Little Stanmore, Edgware, Kingsbury, Hendon and Pinner. The Board of Guardians set up to administer the Union included four from Harrow and two from Pinner. The Union's assets included the four parish workhouses at Harrow, Pinner, Great Stanmore and Hendon. While considering the best way to utilise these properties the guardians caused the most vulnerable inhabitants of this part of Middlesex to be shuttled about the union in a shameful way. They pro-

86. A view of West Street and the old workhouse in the early twentieth century.

posed in May 1835[17] that the aged, decayed and respectable poor should be housed at Hendon and that lying-in women, children and unfortunate females should go to Great Stanmore; the impotent poor were to be at Pinner and the able-bodied poor at Harrow. In August they decided that Harrow workhouse 'should be kept unoccupied for the present to ascertain whether it will be required during the coming winter' and that the inmates should be sent to other houses. They then decreed that the poor from Stanmore should be moved to Hendon and the poor from Pinner to Stanmore so that both Pinner and Harrow workhouses could be 'kept ready in case of an influx of able-bodied poor during the winter'. There was yet another scheme for converting the Harrow house into an infirmary for the Union. All came to nothing as the guardians eventually realised that a new central workhouse was necessary and started looking for a suitable site in the autumn of 1837. In October 1838 a field at Redhill was purchased from Mr Gares and the contract for building the Union Workhouse went to Mr Charles Tenter in September 1839. It was ready in the summer of 1840.

APPRENTICESHIP

Great efforts were made to apprentice poor children to prevent them from being a burden on the parish and to give them a trade to maintain themselves as adults. The overseers, with the consent of two justices, could bind poor boys until they were 24 and girls until the age of 21 or their marriage if that came earlier, irrespective of the age at which the children were bound. From 1780 the boys also could only be apprenticed to the age of 21 years. The parish paid a premium to the master who then wholly maintained the child. Between 1740-80 Harrow overseers obliged the masters to enter into a bond agreeing not to free the children before the full term had expired. The system was clearly open to abuse, unless the overseers inquired carefully into the character of the masters and kept in touch with the children.

An entry made in the Harrow Vestry Minute Book in 1707[18] shows that the overseers were happy to shift responsibility for apprentices. Mr Brian, headmaster of Harrow School, was anxious (like many other parishioners at the time) to build a pew for himself and family in the south aisle of St Mary's and applied to the vestry for leave to do so in December 1706. His application was granted on condition that he put a poor parish boy to apprentice and the following March it was noted that he had bound out John, the son of John Wilde and expended as much as he was obliged. He got his pew, but what became of John Wilde?

From 1648 the Governors of Harrow School fulfilled part of their obligations under the will of John Lyon to expend profits on charitable purposes by paying premiums for poor children.[19] Between 1648 and 1871 the school assisted some 600 children, mainly boys until 1833 and thereafter nearly equal numbers of both sexes. This charity saved the ratepayers a vast amount of money, as the parish bound out only 89 children between 1705-1833. Most premiums were £5, but occasionally £3 or £4, throughout the long period.

Those bound by the Governors of the School seem to have fared better than the parish apprentices, being bound for a term of years (usually seven), rather than to age 24 and in practically all cases to skilled trades. The only exceptions were in 1725 when seven of the nine children were designated 'poor child' and bound until 21 or 24. Maybe this indicates that the governors assisted children of poor parents who could not afford premiums, but not usually those 'on the parish'. Nor was any distinction made between the sons of humble labourers and husbandmen and those of tradesmen and craftsmen. The son of John Robinson, husbandman who was bound to a Merchant Tailor of London in 1677 is one of many instances. A significant number of the parish children were apprenticed to such trades as farming, husbandmen, warehousemen and housewifery, which promised little in the way of future advancement. The most popular trades were shoemakers, carpenters, blacksmiths and tailors, but boys were also apprenticed to an ivory turner, a goldbeater, needlemaker, comb maker and lorimers (harness maker).[20] Dressmakers and mantua makers and milliners regularly took the girls.[21] Only one child, Thomas Read, a 10-year-old orphan, was apprenticed, by the parish, to that most dreadful of all trades, chimney sweeping, for a period of six years in 1833.[22]

The average age of apprenticeship (where the age is known) was 12 and a half. The youngest was Myrtilla Kirton who was 9 in 1747 when she was apprenticed to housewifery at Henry Golder's house at New Brentford. Three years later her 10-year-old brother, Isaac, followed her to the same household to be a husbandman.

Although none of the children were sent to the other end of the country, they were scattered across the whole of the county of Middlesex and out to Penn and Amersham in Buckinghamshire, St Albans in Hertfordshire, Kingston-upon-Thames in Surrey and Bexley in Kent; places sufficiently distant from Harrow to effectively cut them off from friends or family. However, a significant number were apprenticed within the hamlets of Harrow parish, especially in Harrow Weald and some to their own fathers and occasionally mothers. Some did well and names appear about 20 years apart as first apprentices, then as masters. William Butterfield, apprenticed to Edmund Goshawk, hairdresser and taxidermist, later took on Goshawk's son as an apprentice at his hairdresser's establishment in Bryanston Square.[23]

1   LMA: LA/HA 47.
2   LMA: Acc 76/2019.
3   LMA: LA/HW 47.
4   *Ibid.*
5   *Ibid.*
6   LMA: DRO 3/C1/1.
7   *Ibid.*
8   *Ibid.*
9   LMA: LA/HW 47.
10 *Ibid.*
11 LMA: DRO 3/C1/1.
12 *Ibid.*
13 *Ibid.*
14 *Ibid.*
15 *Ibid.*
16 LMA: DRO 3/C1/4.
17 This section is based on information in Hendon Board of Guardians Minute Books: LMA: BGH/1 and 2.
18 LMA: DRO 3/C1/1.
19 Golland Jim: *The Harrow Apprentices,* 1981.
20 *Ibid.*
21 *Ibid.*
22 *Ibid.*
23 *Ibid.*

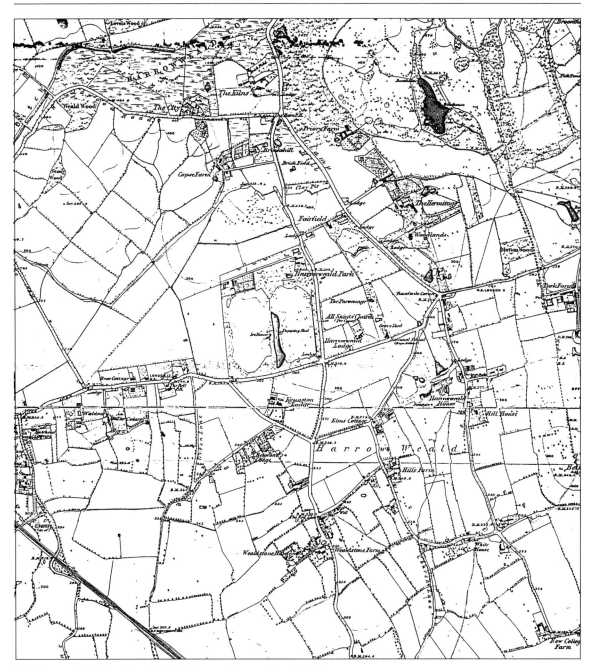

87. Harrow Weald on the six inch Ordnance Survey Map 1864-5.

Developments in Harrow Weald

Harrow Weald as shown on Benjamin Hare's map of 1614[1] – woodland dotted with wastehold cottages to the north, and farm houses and cottages lying on the southern fringes of the common which extended south to the modern College Road – was transformed during the eighteenth and early nineteenth century into a desirable rural retreat studded with gentlemen's houses set amid parkland and landscaped gardens. In the late eighteenth century a few gentry houses began to appear on the eastern side of the common, between what is now Clamp Hill and the parish boundary with Great Stanmore, south of the lands of Bentley Priory, replacing cottages shown on the Hare map. The hillside situation was attractive and like Stanmore Hill

and Common close by, appealed to gentlemen with business in London because of the easy journey to town down the Edgware Road. Travel became faster and perhaps more comfortable after the London & Birmingham Railway Company drove a railway line across the parish in 1837, opening Harrow Station (now Harrow & Wealdstone Station) the same year and Pinner Station (now Hatch End Station) in 1842.

BENTLEY PRIORY

After the dissolution of the monasteries in the sixteenth century the lands of the medieval priory passed to the Colte family for about eighty years and then to the Coghills for about seventy years. Nothing is known of the mansion at that period, but the house now called Lower Priory Farm off Clamp Hill is probably close to the site of the old chapel and may originally have been constructed from its materials. About 1780 James Duberly, then owner, built a fine new house much higher up the hill which forms the basis

88. Bentley Priory. The clock tower was added during Sir John Kelk's ownership.

of the present Bentley Priory, which he soon sold to the first Marquess of Abercorn (1756-1817).[2] He was a rather dashing character, whose Spanish complexion earned him the sobriquet, Don Whiskerandos, from Richard Brinsley Sheridan. He lost his first wife to consumption, divorced his second wife after she eloped with his first wife's brother and although married a third time, attended assemblies surrounded by a bevy of young beauties, all scantily clad, but in the classical style. He set Sir John Soane to improve his house between 1788-99. Already in 1795 Lysons was able to describe it as 'a noble mansion in which convenience is united with magnificence'. About the time of his third marriage in 1810 the Marquess instigated further alterations and extensions, this time by Robert Smirke, then a young architect, whose work may have caused Brewer in his *Beauties of England & Wales* published in 1816, to dismiss Bentley Priory as 'an irregular range of brick building, destitute of architectural beauty and of rather a gloomy character'.

The varied company of Georgian and Regency politicians, actors, writers and exiled royalty who were entertained there included Pitt and Canning, Sheridan, Mrs Siddons and Kemble, Nelson's mistress, Lady Hamilton, and the Princess of Wales. Lady Morgan claimed that 120 people, not counting the underservants, slept there one Christmas holiday and that the place was more like a little town than a house.[3]

George Harley Drummond (1783-1855) great-grandson of the founder of Drummond's Bank at Charing Cross and owner of Stanmore Park, having bought the New College farm on Clamp Hill and having also acquired several head tenements and Kenton Lane Farm in Harrow Weald, held a swathe of land running south from Bent-

ley Priory and marching with Stanmore Park on the east. He emerged as a very large landowner in Harrow at the time of the Enclosure Award, second only to Lord Northwick, but alas, he was a gambler and is credited with having lost £20,000 to Beau Brummell in a single sitting at White's. By 1816 he had leased out Stanmore Park and retired to Drumtochty to repair his losses. The second Marquess of Abercorn bought Stanmore Park in 1839 and Kenton Lane Farm in 1840. By 1852 Bentley Priory had 1344 acres, of which 800 lay in Harrow parish.[4]

The second Marquess of Abercorn also got into financial difficulties and leased the house to Queen Adelaide, widow of William IV, in 1848. She was in frail health and had been advised that the air at the Priory was 'salubrious'. She died there in 1849 and Abercorn sold his local property between 1852-6. Bentley Priory went to Sir John Kelk, the railway engineer who remodelled it on Italianate lines and added the clock tower which now makes the house a landmark for miles around. Kenton Lane Farm was sold to St Bartholomew's Hospital in 1856,[5] which retained it until selling the land to Kenton Estates Ltd for building development in 1930.

The last private owner of Bentley Priory was the flamboyant hotelier and restaurateur, Frederick Gordon, who took it over from Kelk in 1881 and converted it into a grand country-house style hotel in 1885, making much play in his brochure of the royal connection, even though he seems to have turned the royal bedchamber into new kitchens. Mr Gordon formed the Harrow & Stanmore Railway Company which opened a station in Old Church Lane, Stanmore, with the express purpose of enabling hotel guests to arrive from 'town' with speed and in comfort, but they failed to materialise in sufficient numbers and the hotel did not prosper. The Gordon family took up residence again, but sometimes lived in a house he had built in the grounds called Glenthorne. After his death the house became a girls' boarding school from 1908-24/5, when the RAF took it over. The Middlesex County Council made 90 acres of the park into green belt land which is now the Bentley Priory Open Space, while some of the land near to the Uxbridge Road was developed with housing.

89. Lower Priory Farm, Clamp Hill which is perhaps close to the site of the old Bentley Priory chapel.

THE WOODLANDS AND THE HERMITAGE[6]

Two other houses were built on the edge of the common east of Clamp Hill about 1780. One called The Woodlands was the home of William Martin and seems to have first been situated on the site of a cottage shown as William Jackett's on the Hare map of 1614, when it was an encroachment on the waste. By 1807, having acquired more pieces of waste, about five and a half acres altogether, Mr Martin had taken down the first house and was building a new one which was surrounded by a shrubbery. Stephen Kennard, an East India merchant lived there in the 1850s and it belonged to Sir Roger Moon of the London & North Western Railway by 1874. The last private residents, in the 1930s, were Lord and Lady Catto. The house was bought by the council in 1946 and it housed the Engineers' Department until the London Borough of Harrow's new Civic Centre was ready in 1973. The house was demolished the following year and the site sold to the North West Metropolitan Hospital Board for a hospital for the mentally and physically handicapped. A private nursing home stands on the site in the year 2000 with a splendid cedar from the old grounds standing in front of it.

John Philip Kemble, the actor who was friend of the first Marquess of Abercorn, lived in a house called St Leonards a little higher up the hill. He sold it to the Marquess in 1798, who

91. The Woodlands, Clamp Hill, was built by William Martin, c.1807, to replace an earlier house on the edge of the waste.

shortly afterwards purchased the piece of common lying between the house and Clamp Hill. It was renamed The Hermitage and was owned by a solicitor called Richard Hole by 1850. The rather splendid, though now greatly enlarged, lodge which still stands in Clamp Hill, decorated with medieval heads, possibly dates from this time. Later owners included Lt Col Alexander Winch and Sir Reginald Blair who was MP for Bromley and Bow from 1912-22 and for Hendon 1935-45. He and his wife lived there from 1908-25. The house was demolished in the 1930s. Heriots Wood Grammar School for girls opened in the grounds in 1956. It is now Bentley Wood High School. This house should not be confused with the other Hermitage in Kenton Lane.

90. Hermitage Gate in Clamp Hill is the lodge to the Hermitage which stood in what are now the grounds of Bentley Wood High School.

THE BLACKWELL FAMILY'S HOUSES[7]

The Blackwell family name is still prominent in Harrow Weald, with the Blackwell Hall beside All Saints' church, the Cedars Community Centre in the grounds of their former house, the Cedars, near the Uxbridge Road, Oxhey Lane and Courtenay Avenue roundabout and a memorial entrance to the Harrow Weald Recreation Ground in Box Tree Lane which Thomas Francis Blackwell presented to the parish. Hatch End High School was formerly named after the Blackwells.

Thomas Blackwell the younger son of Charles and Mary of the Kiln (*see* pp 60-3), was apprenticed to West & Wyatt, oilmen, of King Street, Soho in 1819. Edmund Crosse was a fellow apprentice and when Mr Wyatt retired in 1829,

92.   The Cedars was built for Thomas Francis Blackwell, c.1868, to the designs of Robert Lewis Roumieu.   It was on the site of the former Clock House.   Demolition started in 1957.   Only the gates and curved flanking railings survive.

they bought the business together and made it into the famous Crosse & Blackwell's.   When Thomas married Jane Bernasconi in 1834 they first lived in Bedford Square, then above the business when it moved to Soho Square in 1839. Edmund Crosse and his wife lived there too. Both families soon had country residences at Harrow Weald.   Thomas Blackwell built Brookshill, which was later called The Hall, a little south of The Hare public house, near the top of Brookshill and Edmund Crosse built

93.   Oak Lodge, Brookshill.

Fairfield lower down the slope, between Brookshill and Clamp Hill about 1844.   Fairfield ended its days as the Belgrano social and residential club which opened there in 1938.   Brookshill was used as a hospital during the First World War, became a nursing home in 1935 and was demolished in 1967.   A lodge remains in Brookshill.

Thomas Blackwell's parents-in-law, the Bernasconis, had a residence at Harrow Weald which became The Cedars, but was originally called the Clock House.   It stood on the site of a cottage, designated Dolor's House on the Hare map and in the possession of William Spittle at the time of the enclosure.   Thomas and Jane Blackwell's eldest surviving son, Thomas Francis Blackwell, took it over in 1868 and had the house rebuilt in a Gothic style to the designs of Robert Lewis Roumieu.   The architect was married to Thomas Francis Blackwell's wife's sister and he eventually died at the Cedars in 1877.   His son, Reginald St Aubyn Roumieu designed some houses in Westfield Park, Hatch End, for the Blackwells in 1892.

Mrs Blackwell died shortly before the Second World War, and the Cedars was acquired by the LCC for a housing estate.   It was hoped that the house would be used as a community centre, but it was requisitioned by the government during the war.   Demolition came in 1957 and the

94. Hillside in Brookshill after the fire which left it in a precarious state. This house, designed by Robert Lewis Roumieu, was built for Charles Blackwell's widow and her daughters. It is dated 1868.

Community Centre now on the site is a strictly utilitarian prefabricated building. The grounds became a public open space, complete with cedars, and the gates made by the Bromsgrove Guild, gate piers and curved flanking railings which survive were listed as a sop to conservationists. A pair of attractive cottages remain on the opposite side of the road, one of which, now much altered, was the laundry and there are other staff cottages on the north side of the Uxbridge Road.

Thomas and Jane Blackwell's eldest son, Charles, died young leaving a widow and three daughters. This family lived for a time at Brookshill with the older Blackwells and are listed there in the 1871 census, but moved to Hillside, built for them by Thomas Blackwell near by in Brookshill. R.L. Roumieu was again the architect. The 1881 census shows that the family at Hillside then had four servants, a gardener at Hillside Cottage and a coachman at Hillside Stables. The youngest of the daughters, Helen Bertha Blackwell, died in May 1955 and the house was bought at auction by Mr Ross in

1958. Tramps broke in shortly afterwards and set it on fire, since when the house has remained in a precarious state. A member of the Ross family runs a riding school from the stables. The house and site is in constant demand, but schemes to have a nursing home there and a religious meeting room have all failed because of tremendous local opposition. Its future is still uncertain.

95. Hillside stables.

96. Harrow Weald Park built by William Windale early in the nineteenth century; from a sales catalogue of 1858.

HARROW WEALD PARK[8]

Harrow Weald Park stood on Brooks Hill in extensive grounds of 53 acres, which before the enclosure was part of the common. William Windale of Mayor's Court Office, London, purchased 26 acres, bounded by Brookshill and the Uxbridge Road, from the enclosure commissioners in 1805. He built the house on the highest land and created an elongated lake along his western fence. In 1822 he doubled the size of his grounds in a deed of exchange with the vicar of Harrow who had tithe land all around. Elaborate staff cottages, a laundry and a home farm were built in the north-western corner and most of the grounds were laid out as parkland with gardens near the house. The entrance was at the corner of Brookshill and the Uxbridge Road, between a pair of lodges. The gate piers still stand.

William Crockford (1775-1844), a fishmonger who founded Crockford's Club in 1827 and quickly became a millionaire, lived at Harrow Weald Park for the last four years of his life. The estate was sold by auction in 1858 to Robert Smith, an East India merchant. The next owner in 1867 was a timber merchant, Alexander Sim, whose fancy led him to encase the brickwork of the house in massive stone to produce a castellated effect. The great hall had a hammer beam roof and organ gallery, whilst the ballroom ceiling was a copy of Wolsey's oratory at Hampton Court. The architect, Robert Frere, had been influenced by Charles Barry who worked on the gothic Houses of Parliament until his death, and one wonders whether Roumieu, who was designing the Cedars for Charles F. Blackwell at about the same time, was similarly influenced.

97. Outbuildings forming part of the Harrow Weald Park estate.

98. Harrow Weald Park as altered by Alexander Sim c.1870. It was demolished in 1956.

100. The gamekeeper's cottage on Uxbridge Road is one of a pair of estate cottages belonging to Harrow Weald Park.

99. The coach house of Harrow Weald Park which stands at the top of West Drive.

101. The castellated North Lodge of Harrow Weald Park which still stands in Brookshill.

102. Harrow Weald Lodge, Uxbridge Road, was known as Coldharbour House until the middle of the nineteenth century. It is on the site of the Nag's Head.

Alexander Sim's widow sold the house to an American millionaire, John Hughes, whose son, Harry, was a well-known singer at local concerts. Mr Hughes enjoyed a peaceful retirement driving trotters from his stables around the countryside. The British Israel Society which taught that the British nation is one of the lost tribes of Israel, took over the house in 1932, and part of the park was developed as Park Drive. The society closed down in 1938 and the house was used by the Post Office during the Second World War. It survived until 1956, when it was demolished and replaced by an old people's home. West Drive was built to the west of the lake and leads to the old laundry, stables and cottages which survive as a semi-rural enclave up an unmade track.

HARROW WEALD LODGE[9]
Harrow Weald Lodge, standing on the north side of the Uxbridge Road close to All Saints' Church, is apparently on the site of an inn called the Nag's Head which had changed its name to Coldharbour by 1759 as shown on the Messeder map. The handsome eighteenth-century house has a pediment over the projecting central bays and late eighteenth-century additions on either side. It was known as Coldharbour House into the middle of the nineteenth century, but was sold as Harrow Weald Lodge in 1868, when the sales brochure mentions a shrubbery, coach house, stables, poultry houses and a walled garden, along with two pieces of meadow. Mr Charles Grey Mott lived there with his family

from before 1887-1905. He was chairman and director of several railway companies. The last private owners were Mr and Mrs Brown who stayed there until 1937. It was bought from Mr M.P. Brown by the council in 1941 and has miraculously survived, albeit as offices and with a modern block in red brick built alongside.

HARROW WEALD HOUSE & HARROW WEALD FARM[10]
The Harrow Weald House estate was created in the nineteenth century, out of a number of old enclosures between Kenton Lane and College Hill Road. Several of the pre-enclosure cottages were demolished to create a park and the house, which has an early nineteenth century appearance, may have been developed from one of them. One timber-framed cottage was retained and used as a bailiff's cottage with outbuildings described in a sale brochure of 1914 as 'a farmery'. That house now enlarged is called Harrow Weald House Farm and lies back from Elms Road. The oldest part is a four bay structure dating from about 1600, which has arched braced tie beams, collar beams and through purlins. There is a later timber-framed extension at the west end and a nineteenth century portion.

The estate may have been created by the Revd John Roberts, vicar of Harrow at the time of the enclosure, as it was put up for sale by his trustees in 1870, advertised as having an ornamental water and 'a view of Harrow's noble spire'. Henry Grinling, a wine merchant, came in 1887, and increased its size by buying The Chestnuts in

College Hill Road and some meadow land to the south, so that the estate entirely filled the area between Elms Road, College Hill Road and Kenton Lane and included the forge in Kenton Lane The house became the Whitegate School for girls in 1935. It closed in 1987 and the Westminster House Nursing Home opened there in 1992.

KYNASTON COURT

Among other large houses built on the newly enclosed common was Kynaston Lodge on the north side of Boxtree Lane, which was owned in the mid-nineteenth century, by William Kynaston from Hardwicke Hall, Salop. Later it was called Kynaston Court. The house was sold to the council and the grounds to a developer about 1930. The Kynaston estate of houses with

sunshine windows was being advertised for sale in 1934. The council sold the house to Feltham Central Properties Ltd in 1969 and it was demolished to make way for further development.

SOUTHFIELD PARK

Southfield Park was formerly known as Dancers because the land had belonged to the prominent Dancer family, one of whose members was Daniel Dancer, a notorious miser. It was probably built in the late 1860s and was the home of Jacob Sahler, a baker, who had been born in Prussia. The house has gone, but a lodge remains.

GRIMSDYKE[11]

Perhaps the most architecturally interesting house built in Harrow Weald, is Grimsdyke,

103. The drawing room at Grimsdyke in W.S. Gilbert's time.

104. All Saints Church in recent times.

designed by Richard Norman Shaw and built 1870-2 for Frederick Goodall, the Royal Academician. It was erected just south of the ancient earthwork which runs through the grounds and is a large, but picturesque building with many gables and decorated with half timbering and ornamental tiles. He used it as a studio and for entertaining. His guests enjoyed feeding dates to the desert sheep and goats which he brought back to Grimsdyke from his travels in the Middle East and featured in his paintings. W.S. Gilbert of Gilbert & Sullivan fame, bought it in 1890 and had the house extended by Ernest George & Peto. Gilbert died in 1911, from a heart attack brought on by his exertions in swimming out to help a lady who had got into difficulties while bathing in a the lake in the grounds.

When Lady Gilbert died in 1937 the Middlesex County Council bought the estate and the house became a rehabilitation centre for tuberculosis patients. It stood empty for many years after 1962, but was restored and opened as a country house hotel in 1972.

ALL SAINTS CHURCH[12]

Being so far distant from the parish church, it is hardly surprising that the people of Harrow Weald had their own chapel built in 1815 on land owned by the vicar of Harrow, the Revd John Roberts. The site is now occupied by the lych gate and war memorial. As the hamlet developed a larger and more important church was needed and All Saints was begun in 1846, designed by James Park Harrison in Early English style, which did not please everyone. Only his chancel and sacristy were built and William Butterfield completed the work in the more approved Decorated style. The church was consecrated in 1849 and completed in 1852, but the population of the parish continued to expand and the church was practically rebuilt in 1890, again to designs of William Butterfield and mainly due to the generosity of Charles Francis Blackwell. The south aisle and chancel remained unchanged, but the nave roof was raised, and a clerestory and the imposing looking tower were added. A vicarage behind the church and

105. All Saints Church before the alterations of 1890.

a school beside it were both built in 1845.

The first vicar, Edward Monro, founded with the help of his family, St Andrew's College for working men and boys in a cottage, which gave its name to College Hill Road. Mr Munro left for Leeds in 1860, where he saw an even greater need for education for the working classes and sadly the college in Harrow Weald did not long survive his departure.

A small part of Harrow Weald parish was taken into the new parish of Hatch End in 1895, when St Anselm's was opened and the southern portion became part of St Michael and All Angels in 1935.

106. Grimsdyke in 1966.

PROTESTANT NON-CONFORMITY

There was a meeting of Particular Baptists in Harrow Weald from 1846 to at least 1882. The Methodists had a mission room from 1889 to 1935. Later they met at All Saints.

[1] LMA: Acc 892.

[2] *Victoria County History, Middlesex*, Vol IV.

[3] Druett, W W. *The Stanmores and Harrow Weald through the ages* (1938).

[4] Harrow Central Reference Library: Bentley Priory Sales Particulars 1880.

[5] St Bartholomew's Hospital Archives: Governor's Journal 1854-60.

[6] Information from Harrow Central Reference Library: House Files.

[7] Information from Druett: *op. cit* and Harrow Central Reference Library: House Files and notes of Blackwell Family.

[8] Harrow Central Reference Library: Sales Catalogues and House Files.

[9] Harrow Central Reference Library: House Files.

[10] Harrow Central Reference Library: Sales Catalogues and House Files.

[11] Cherry & Pevsner: *The Buildings of England: London 3, North West* (1991).

[12] Jenkins N. *All Saints Harrow Weald, a short history* (1990).

Wealdstone

THE WEALD STONE

The southern portion of Weald, largely where the open fields of the hamlet had been before enclosure, had become industrial Wealdstone by the end of the nineteenth century. The weald stone from which the area takes its name is to be found outside a public house which was called the Lion or Red Lion for at least two hundred years, but became The Wealdstone Inn in 1996. The present building is modern. Photographs of its predecessor show that the weald stone was built into the walls. Like many sarsens (fused mica of Eocene age occurring in the Reading Beds which underlie the London clay), it was probably used as a wayside marker on the boundary of the weald or wood. Rocque's map of Middlesex 1754 is the first to mark the area where Weald Lane and College Road meet the High Road, as Wealdstone. On the corner of

108. *The Red Lion seen here was replaced by the present building in the 1930s. The name of the pub was changed to The Wealdstone Inn in 1996.*

Weald Lane stood Wealdstone House, another of the Dancer family's properties. Francis Dancer, farmer, occupied it in 1850. The house was sold in 1873 with four and a half acres and was

107. *Wealdstone as shown on the six-inch Ordnance Survey map of 1868.*

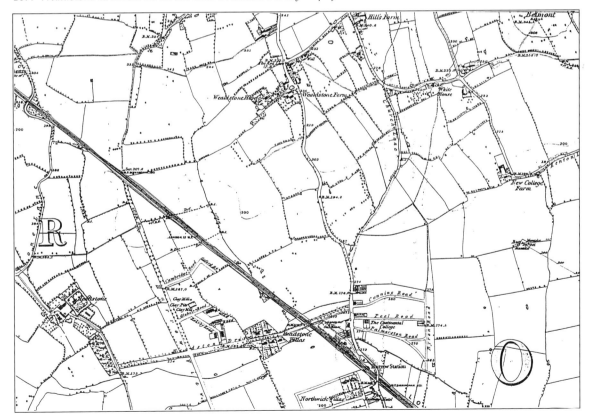

described as 'pleasantly close to the village of Harrow Weald'. It was a sixteenth century house given a brick facade and cornice in the eighteenth century and further altered later. H.P. Cobb, a Radical politician, purchased it in 1878. It was demolished in 1947. Wealdstone Farm on the south side of Weald Lane disappeared between 1894 and 1913.

THE RAILWAY

Harrow was on the route of the London & Birmingham Railway Company's line which opened as far as Boxmoor in July 1837. Although the company's aim was to develop traffic between the midlands and London, rather than create suburbia, intermediate stations were built and Harrow Station, the first one out of Euston, opened the same year. Its position amid green fields two miles from Harrow Town may be due to the governors of Harrow School wishing to preserve their territory from future development, but it is more likely that Robert Stephenson, the engineer, refused to lay lines up gradients of more than one in three hundred and thirty. Compensation was paid to the owners of farmland taken by the railway, Francis Dancer receiving £33 16s. The London & Birmingham Railway Company amalgamated with others to become the London & North Western Railway in 1846. In 1923 it became the London, Midland & Scottish Railway until becoming part of British Rail in 1948. A suburban line from Harrow to Watford

110. Wealdstone House, the home of Francis Dancer in 1850. The eighteenth-century façade and cornice hide a much earlier timber-framed house.

operated from 1913 and was electrified in 1917. The station itself was completely rebuilt in 1911 to the designs of Gerald Horsley. Hatch End Station by the same architect was rebuilt at the same time.

The saddest incident in connection with the station is the tragic rail disaster on Wednesday 8 October 1952. The Perth express heading south, having unaccountably passed red signals, ran into the rear of a local train from Tring that was standing at the platform at 8.19 in the morning. As the express slewed across the lines a train bound for Liverpool collided with it. 122 people were killed and 157 injured. Many local people assisted with the rescue work which continued until the Friday evening.

CITY OF LONDON & COUNTIES FREEHOLD LAND SOCIETY

The area around the station became known as Station End, but there were no developments until 1854 when the City of London and Counties Freehold Land Society bought land near the station and laid out the Harrow Park estate consisting of Canning, Peel, Palmerston and Byron Roads. The section of High Road joining them was meant to have been called Pitt Terrace, but the name never caught on. The street names alone, of politicians and a poet who all supported ideas of parliamentary reform in some measure, give a clue to the Society's aim, which was to enfranchise working men by helping them to obtain freehold property valued at 40 shillings a year – then the necessary property qualification for entitlement to vote in the county elections. The 220 plots into which the area was divided varied

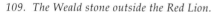

109. The Weald stone outside the Red Lion.

111. An LNWR horse bus outside the original Harrow and Wealdstone Station in the 1890s.

in price between £30 and £65 and buyers were bound to build houses between £200 and £800 in value. Maybe the Society expected city clerks (one thinks of Mr Pooter) and their families to move out to Harrow, because purchasers of plots costing £50 and more were entitled to educate their sons at Harrow School and received a first class ticket between Harrow and Euston for eleven years. Residents of the Woodridings estate which was being developed near Pinner Station (now Hatch End) between 1855-61 received first class travel for 13 years!

The Harrow Park estate did not 'take off', perhaps because the mixture of house sizes did not appeal to the type of person who was prepared to live so far from work. All the plots on the Woodridings estate were worth more than £50 and the villa residences there had attracted lawyers, London merchants and civil servants, not to mention Mr & Mrs Beeton of cookery book fame, by the time of the 1861 census. That pattern was not followed in Wealdstone where the 25-inch Ordnance Survey map of 1864 shows that scarcely any building had taken place by then, only about eight houses having been erected on the High Road frontage and a school called the Continental College between Peel and Palmerston Roads. Houses gradually filled in the spaces from about 1870. Some small workshops grew up in these streets interspersed among the houses.

INDUSTRY

In 1886 the first of the industrial concerns came to Wealdstone, Cogswell and Harrison, gunsmiths, who stayed only until 1894 because of a fire, perhaps caused by sparks from the railway, which destroyed their premises. They were followed in 1890 by the Eastman Photographic Company (later Kodak); Allen Bros. and George Pulman & Sons, both printers, in 1896 and 1901; Winsor & Newton (fine arts) in 1897; Hamilton's Brush Works in 1898 and Ingall, Parsons, Clive and Co.'s Coffin Factory in 1900. Whitefriars Glassworks moved from the City in 1923, providing about 250 jobs. Ingalls & Parson's had come from Birmingham, and Hamilton's from Clerkenwell. What could have brought them? Initially there were no utilities apart from gas, which was supplied from the gas works opened in 1855 by John Chapman of Roxeth. There was a gasometer in Wealdstone by 1864. Water, however, was abundant, there being five artesian wells on the Kodak site.

Maybe the railway with its easy access to coal and other raw materials from the north and midlands and markets in London and beyond was the main attraction, but why had it failed to appeal during the first fifty or sixty years of its existence? The still rural landscape with plenty of room for expansion may have been the deciding factor. Kodak originally had some idea

112. Kodak site viewed from the corner of Milton Road and Marlborough Hill.

of producing gelatine from cattle and certainly spread far beyond its original seven acres to the present day 55 acres. Although electricity was supplied to Harrow Town in 1894, it was not laid on in Wealdstone until 1906, so Eastman (Kodak) had its own power station fired by coal and Hamilton's had a steam engine driving a dynamo to generate electricity. Winsor & Newton relied upon a gas engine fuelled with anthracite to power a system of shafts and leather belts. A telephone exchange opened in 1905.

Apart from Kodak and Winsor & Newton, which now trades as Colart Fine Arts & Graph-

ics, these concerns which once animated the Wealdstone scene and employed so many of its people, have closed or moved elsewhere. Whitefriars production ceased in September 1980. Allen Brothers' premises were first taken over by Waterlow & Sons, then became the HMSO Printing Works during the war and closed at the end of 1982, in preparation for its move to Norwich. The Meteorological Office came in 1946 and was situated behind the HMSO. The Star Brush Company joined with Hamilton's and employed 300 workers in the 1970s, but closed at the end of 1990. The coffin factory became a storage depot for Schweppes.

WEALDSTONE HILL ESTATE AND OTHER HOUSING

The population doubled between each census from 1881-1911: starting at 1240 in 1881 and rising to 2504 in 1891; to 5901 in 1901; and to 11,923 in 1911. Some of the families lived in new houses on the Wealdstone Hill Estate (Grant, Thomson and Stirling Roads), built on land bought from the Dean and Chapter of Christ Church, Oxford, by the London Land Association. The plots were sold at public auction and by private treaty between April 1898 and July 1899 and bought by white collar workers. On

113. Harrow and Wealdstone Station as rebuilt in 1911 to the designs of Gerald Horsley. The initials of the London and North Western Railway can still be seen beneath the parapet.

114. Holy Trinity designed by Charles Roumieu and Aitchison, built in 1881.

the opposite side of the High Road working class houses were arising in Gordon, Havelock, Wellington and Graham Roads.

CHURCHES AND OTHER AMENITIES

By the time the First World War broke out Wealdstone was a complete town in its own right and was indeed an Urban District from 1895-1934, when it became a ward within a newly enlarged Harrow Urban District. It had achieved a public hall of corrugated iron (1892); a fire station manned by volunteers (1896); a police station and court house where W.S. Gilbert sat on the bench (1909); and several churches. Charles St Aubyn Roumieu and his partner Aitchison designed Holy Trinity Church, which was built in 1881 and enlarged in 1903 as the population grew.

The Society of Protestant Dissenters called Particular or Calvinistic Baptists met from 1875 in a room over a carpenter's shop and opened

Station End Chapel in Palmerston Road in 1879. Having greatly increased in numbers they moved to the public hall in 1901 which was renamed the Wealdstone Baptist Church Hall in 1903. A brand new chapel was built just to the north and opened in 1905. It flourished and had 700 children attending the Sunday School in 1930. The old Station End Chapel was taken over by the Salvation Army.

The Methodists had meetings in a brewery store in 1883 and built a Mission Hall in the High Road in 1885. After using a school hall for two or three years when more accommodation was needed, a new church was erected in Locket Road in 1905. The 'tin hut' was dismantled and became a refreshment pavilion at a tea-garden in Ruislip. The Primitive Wesleyans also had a Mission Hall, on the corner of Gordon Road and the High Street which became a YMCA in 1917.

The Catholic mission was established in Wealdstone in 1899 with mass being offered once a month in the Public Hall, which had been erected in the High Road in 1892. A group of Salvatorian Fathers from Germany took a house called Avondale between Claremont and Risingholme Roads in 1901, moved to the Elms nearby the next year and finally opened a tin church, complete with belfry in 1906. This continued in use as a school until 1954, the present church of St Joseph by Adrian Gilbert Scott having been opened in 1931. The Salvatorians opened a parish school in another tin hut in 1908. French nuns came to run the parish school and had established the Sacred Heart High School as well by 1907. The grammar school for boys known as Salvatorian College opened in 1926 and has since expanded over the site beside the church.

115. St Joseph's Roman Catholic church was opened in 1931. The architect was Adrian Gilbert Scott.

116. The Police Station and Magistrates' Court in Wealdstone High Street, designed by J. Dixon Butler. The court house opened in 1909.

117. *The Garraway family's cabs pose outside The Case is Altered in Wealdstone c.1900. There are three public houses with this unusual name within a few miles of each other; at Harrow Weald, here at Wealdstone and at Eastcote.*

118. Harrow Civic Centre 1972, designed by Eric Broughton in association with the Borough Architect. It was built on the site of Poets' Corner.

POETS' CORNER TO CIVIC CENTRE

The 1864 OS map shows a few houses named Northwick Villas built in what became Marlborough Road just behind the Railway Hotel, and Marlborough Hill laid out as a road, though not named. From the mid-1870s a group of roads named after poets, Milton, Burns, Shelley and Wordsworth, had begun to be developed on the field to the south of Marlborough Hill and bounded on the east by Marlborough Road. This area, known as Poets' Corner, was designated as a Comprehensive Development Area in the Middlesex Development Plan of 1951. Nearly all the properties were considered obsolete from age or poor condition and they would be cleared away to provide a site for a Civic Centre. There had been plans for such a centre ever since the Harrow Urban District had come into being in 1934 and various sites had been considered. Poets' Corner was thought to be both central and accessible, so work of clearance and rehousing displaced families began. By the time the Civic Centre was opened in November 1972, the Harrow Urban District Council had been superseded by the London Borough of Harrow.

Sources

Dark, Arthur: *From Rural Middlesex to London Borough,* London Borough of Harrow (1981).

Druett, W.W: *The Stanmores and Harrow Weald through the ages* (1938).

Wilkins, H.M: *The Wealdstone Scene* (1976).

Victoria County History, Middlesex, Vol IV.

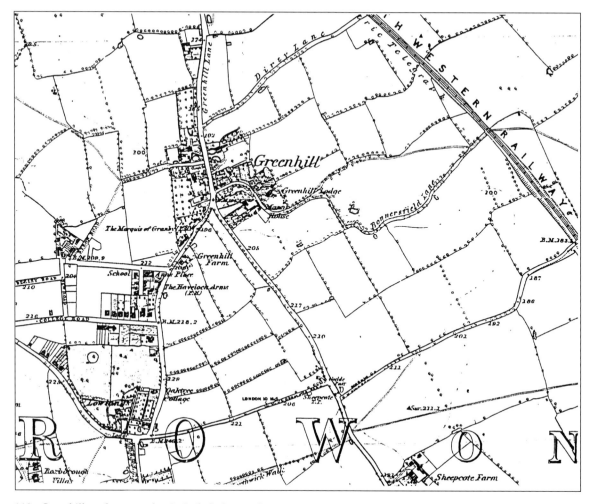

119. *Greenhill as shown on the six-inch Ordnance Survey map 1868.*

Greenhill – Hamlet to Shopping Centre

GREENHILL IN THE 1860s

Immediately south of Wealdstone lies Greenhill, once a quiet hamlet with a few farms and cottages around the junction of what are now Station Road, Sheepcote Road and Bonnersfield Lane. It is now Harrow's main shopping centre. Harrow Metropolitan Line station was opened at the southern end of Greenhill in 1880, placing the hamlet fairly between two fast lines into Town, and leading inevitably to massive devel-

opment of the former farmland during the next thirty years. Some heralds of Greenhill's future were already to be seen in the layout of College, Kymberley, Headstone, Byron and St Ann's Roads on the 1868 six-inch Ordnance Survey map, albeit with scarcely any houses then built. The latter road was then unnamed, but had the Greenhill National School (built in 1859) and three pairs of semi-detached houses called Ann's Place, at the Station Road end. Two lanes, Dirty Lane (now Elmgrove Road) and Bonnersfield Lane, branched off to the east of Greenhill Lane (now Station Road) leading to the former open fields.

The earliest houses still standing in the 1860s, were situated in Bonnersfield Lane. They were called the Manor House and Greenhill Lodge,

120. Mrs Elda Gibbs at Ann's Place. The cottages were replaced by the Harrow Observer offices in 1960.

and are probably identifiable with head tenements mentioned in the 1547 survey. A little further north on either side of the green were Fairholme Farm (just north of the present Fairholme Road) and The Crofts, both dating from the mid-eighteenth century. Greenhill Farm, unnamed on the map, stood further south on the west side of Station Road on the site now occupied by the Safari Cinema and Tesco, although the map rather confusingly names a group of buildings at the junction of the present Lyon Road and Station Road as Greenhill Farm. The Marquis of Granby, known as The Six Bells from

1746 until 1775, and a smithy stood in Station Road near a timber-framed cottage called Kenmare (the whole site now occupied by Debenham's) and the Havelock Arms was near Ann's Place. On the east side of what is now Peterborough Road lay Oak Tree Cottage, opposite a large house called Lowlands which was set in extensive grounds (now Harrow College).

LOWLANDS

An intriguing entry in Thomas Smith's *Handbook for the use of visitors to Harrow-on-the-Hill*, published in 1850, is that of Anthony H. Gibson, bath-keeper. His baths and douches on the hydropathic principle were situated in the grounds at Lowlands and had been installed by the owner, Benjamin Rotch (1793-1854) who had moved there with his wife, Isabella, in 1827. He was a barrister, but was keen on modern innovations and had an inventive mind. Presumably he let the baths to Mr Gibson, who opened them to the public.

Mr Rotch had chambers in Furnival's Inn and a house close by in the parish of St Andrew's, Holborn. He was active on committees considering new methods of prison organisation, the design of the new prison at Clerkenwell and also Colney Hatch Lunatic Asylum, in addition to being chairman of the Middlesex Quarter Sessions from 1833-5 and a magistrate in the Gore Division.[1] There is an unsubstantiated story that he utilised the lodge at Lowlands as a court house where he dealt summarily with local offenders. His widow lived on at Lowlands until her death at the age of 100 in 1909. On the 1861 census enumerator's sheet, she appears as a 'gentlewoman', born in Stamford. Her widowed mother, also born in Stamford, was living with her and there were two visitors. The staff consisted of a cook, a lady's maid and a labourer. The gardener, Robert Wright and his wife formed a separate household.

The Metropolitan Line ran across the Lowlands estate, but left Mrs Rotch with widespread gardens, well laid out and dotted with exotic trees. She entertained largely at Lowlands, especially people connected with Harrow School. After her death a school was built alongside the house and opened as Harrow County School for Girls in 1914, with Miss Mary Huskisson as headmistress and 133 pupils.[2] The school had a good reputation for encouraging girls into higher education until 1974, when

121. *Lowlands was called Cassetta Cottage when it was built in the early nineteenth century. Harrow County School for Girls opened there in 1914 with new buildings alongside. It is now Harrow College.*

it became a Sixth Form College. It was called Lowlands College until 1987 when it was re-named Greenhill College and on 1 August 1999 it merged with Weald College to become Harrow College.

122. *Harrow-on-the-Hill station opened in 1880 with the main entrance as seen here on the Lowlands Road side because most passengers would approach it from the hill and Roxeth, as Greenhill then had very few houses.*

FARMHOUSES

The Greenhill farmland was nibbled away as road frontages were taken mainly for shops, and streets lined with villas gradually filled the areas behind. The farmhouses remained for a number of years after the land had gone. The first hundred plots of the Greenhill Park Estate, with frontages along Hindes Road and Welldon Crescent were put up for sale in June 1899 and Fairholme Road was built soon after, but Fairholme farmhouse stood until 1936. It had been the home of the Finch family. A diary of William Finch for the year 1781, found under the floorboards when the house was being demolished, showed that sheep were kept in the eighteenth century, on Greenhill Ground and on the common.[3] The Hills had taken over by the time of the enclosure in 1817 and Henry Finch Hill who lived there in 1850, described himself as esquire as well as farmer. The house had passed to the Higgins family in 1902 and Gurney A. Higgins, who found the diary, sold the house for development in 1936.

The Manor House in Bonnersfield Lane, which was farmed by Daniel Clewley in 1850[4], was purchased by Sidney Hunt, partner in the timber yard Hunt and Kennard, in 1888. He died in 1915, but his family lived there until the 1930s and it was demolished in 1937 to make way for the Granada cinema[5] (later Cannon Cinema and now closed). The timber yard was established in 1884 on land farmed by the Hodsdon family and supplied wood for the building trade. Owen Hunt, great-nephew of Sidney, became company director in 1977. Hunt Kennards is still in business in Perivale, but sold the timber yard in Harrow for development in 1989.

Greenhill Farm had been split up by the 1920s. The house had become a Veterinary Surgery, owned by Major F. Stewart Probyn and part of the farm was used by Botanicus, a horticultural firm. Some of the land was let to Wealdstone Football Club in 1922. A barn, let to a syndicate, was described in a letter to the *Harrow Observer* in October 1927, as 'one of the few old landmarks left of the town below the hill'.[6] In the year 2000 the last remnant of rural Greenhill is one barn at Turney's Turbines. The Dominion Cinema was built on another part of the site and opened in 1936. It was converted mainly for Bingo in 1972, by which time it was named the ABC. As the Safari, since 1995, it shows Indian films and the Bingo Club still exists alongside. The football club played its last match on the site in 1991, since when a Tesco store has been built on the field.

Greenhill Lodge was split up into building plots 'suitable for villa residences' which were being sold by auction as part of the Greenhill Lodge and Elmgrove Estate in July 1911.[7]

CHURCHES

As ever, churches flourished in the spreading suburb.

St John the Baptist[8] was built in 1866 as a chapel of ease to St Mary's, the mother church on the hill, due to the energies of the then vicar of Harrow, Wayland Joyce. It was for the convenience of older people who found the steep walk up the hill difficult, but as there were only about 200 people in Greenhill at the time he presumably had an eye to the future. The church was a slightly odd edifice, built of brick with an apse and a separate belfry. Hidden behind elm trees, on the corner of Sheepcote and Station Road, it seated 500 and was served by curates from St Mary's. The Revd Thomas Smith, familiarly known as Tommy, served the church with great energy from 1886 until 1932, a year before his death. First he built a hall next to the church

123. *Our Lady and St Thomas of Canterbury, Roxborough Park, was built in 1894 to replace a temporary church of 1873.*

in Station Road in 1888 calling it Victoria Hall in commemoration of the Queen's Golden Jubilee the previous year. Then he presided over the creation of Greenhill as a separate parish in 1896 and the building of a new church from 1904 to meet the needs of the burgeoning population which by 1901 was about 3000. The imposing stone church consecrated in 1905 was not the end of his dream, as he hoped for a much longer nave and a tower. The extended nave and transepts were complete by 1925 and the foundations of a tower had been laid. Tommy's successor, the Revd H.W. Beck did more work on the chancel and sanctuary, but abandoned the idea of a tower. The church, however, is a fine building and holds its own against the commercial development all around.

Our Lady and St Thomas of Canterbury, built in Roxborough Park in 1873, was the nearest catholic church to Greenhill. This temporary church was replaced in 1894 by the present building which was designed by Arthur Young and contains glass by J.E. Nuttgens, the Harrow artist.[9] Methodists, Presbyterians, Congregationalists and Baptists also moved into Greenhill. The Baptists had had a presence in Harrow from 1806 when they first shared meetings with other dissenters at the house of Joseph Freshwater, a carpenter, on Roxeth Hill (then London Hill). They purchased a chapel from the Pinner Presbyterians in 1812 and re-erected it in Byron Hill Road and there flourished, having about 200 members by the end of the century.

124. The tower of Harrow Baptist Church dominated College Road from 1908 until it was incorporated into the town centre improvements of 1982-4. The present church on the same site is far less visible.

The move to College Road, Greenhill, was made in 1908, as it was becoming clear that the old hamlet was rapidly overtaking Harrow Town as an urban centre. Number one College Road was purchased with a plot alongside and there the Baptists have been ever since, although now in completely new premises on the same site, incorporated into the town centre development in 1984. During the rebuilding, between 1982-4, the Baptists used the former Heathfield School building opposite in College Road, the school having recently moved to Pinner.[10]

The Methodists had also been meeting in cottages on the hill from the beginning of the nineteenth century and by 1810 they had a Sunday School at the shop of Mr Powell, a shoemaker, in West Street. Soon afterwards they opened a chapel for 150 people on London Hill (now Roxeth Hill), moving about 1855 into rather grander premises which included a chapel and a caretaker's house, in Lower Road. Greenhill beckoned,

however, and the Primitive Methodists opened a church in Angel Road on the corner of Welldon Crescent in 1904 whilst the Wesleyans built an elaborate church in Bessborough Road in 1905. The Methodists joined with the Presbyterians and Congregationalists in 1975 to form the United Reformed and Methodist Church, using the former Congregational church in Hindes Road for services. The Bessborough Road church was demolished, but the one on Angel Road, having sheltered the Greek Orthodox community (which is now in Kenton) for a number of years, is now the Welldon Centre.

Trinity Presbyterian church was opened in Station Road in 1906 and the Congregationalist church in Hindes Road in 1904. After the combination of the churches, Trinity was demolished in 1976 and the site, between Woodlands and Elmgrove Roads, is now occupied by the appropriately named Kirkfield House.

MOSQUES AND TEMPLES

An Asian community became established in Harrow in the 1970s. The Central Mosque in Station Road opened in two houses and a grand new mosque in Rosslyn Crescent is at the planning stage. A hut in Vaughan Road was used as a Hindu Temple before the opening of the temple at Kenton.

SCHOOLS AND TECHNICAL COLLEGE

There were innumerable private schools in Greenhill. Among the most well known girls' schools were Heathfield, which had moved from Byron Hill Road to College Road in 1901, and St Margaret's. The latter was opened by the Neumann sisters in Hindes Road in 1902, moved to The Crofts in 1904 and to Sheepcote Road in 1936. The Crofts was demolished and shops built along the frontage and a Territorial Army Centre was opened in the grounds after the school left. Heathfield moved into the former Pinner County School premises at Rayners Lane in 1982, where it remains. St Margaret's combined with the Peterborough College for Girls and as Peterborough and St Margaret's is now in Harrow Weald.

Boys' schools were equally numerous and included E. Ivor Hughes' Buckingham College in Hindes Road, the Boys' High School in Sheepcote Road, founded by E.A. Cave in 1907. There was also a County School for Boys opened on the corner of Gayton and Sheepcote Roads in 1911. The Lower School of John Lyon should have been providing secondary education for local boys under the agreement with the gover-

nors of Harrow School, but had only 140 places, inadequate for the growing population. The Middlesex County Council wished John Lyon to expand, but this idea was blocked by the governors of Harrow School and the Middlesex County Council provided the new school in Greenhill instead. The first headmaster, Ernest Young, transferred from John Lyon. When Harrow education services were reorganised in 1974, Harrow County had an excellent academic reputation and was reluctant to lose its grammar school status and its sixth form. Many staff moved elsewhere and it became Gayton High School in 1975 and Harrow High School in 1999.

HARROW TECHNICAL COLLEGE GROWS INTO WESTMINSTER UNIVERSITY

The Technical College grew out of classes in art and domestic science, started by Marion Hewlett in 1887. She was the daughter of the Medical Officer of Harrow School. Her plans to develop technical education for working boys and girls were encouraged and supported by masters at the school and began at 102 High Street. A purpose-built technical college was opened in 1902 in Station Road opposite the Havelock Arms, partially funded by the Middlesex County Council. The art school side of the establishment became increasingly important and an exhibition hall was added in the 1930s. The Technical College moved to Northwick Park between 1956-7 and the School of Art in 1970. The name constantly changed, first to Harrow College of Higher Education, then to the Polytechnic of Central London in 1990 and finally to the University of Westminster in 1992.

125. The newly-built College of Technology in 1959, which became Harrow College of Technology and Art in 1970.

SHOPS AND TRADE

Shops to supply the new houses soon appeared. 1899 saw some opening in Peterborough Road, and on the Station Road end of St Ann's Road. The Greenhill Estate (Greenhill Road and Greenhill Crescent) was begun in 1899 and shops known as Greenhill Parade were built on the Station Road frontage the following year. The land was owned by Thomas Lilley and William Skinner, who had a boot manufacturers' business in Paddington.[11] Lilley & Skinner's were later known nationwide for their shoe shops. Wright Cooper a baker, confectioner and caterer moved to the Parade from the High Street on the Hill where he had catered famously for school

126. *Miss Marion Hewlett, daughter of the Medical Officer of Harrow School, out of whose classes in art and domestic science the Technical College grew.*

127. New shops in St Ann's Road c.1908.

128. R. Smith's shop window in Peterborough Road in the 1890s proudly advertises an illustrious patron.

129. *The smartly-dressed errand boy looks uncertainly at the camera as he stands outside Rigden's Chemist shop in Peterborough Road.*

leaving breakfasts. He adopted modern technology in his 'Electric Machine Bakery', which was always open for inspection. Above his shop he provided the Gayton Rooms for functions. Apart from the purpose-built shops, several houses in St Ann's Road and Clarendon Road were converted for commercial purposes.

Greenhill was soon to have a department store, Soper's now Debenham's. Mr W.H. Soper, a draper, built it in 1914 along Station Road where the old house, Kenmare, had stood, intending to expand as far as the Marquis of Granby. Unfortunately he died in the influenza epidemic shortly after the ending of the First World War. For a time the store was known as Green & Edwards, but reverted to the original Soper's after becoming a subsidiary of Debenham's in

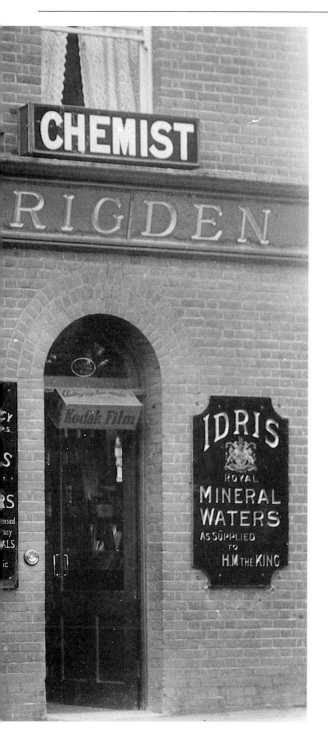

130. An advertisement for Wright Cooper Bros who moved down from the hill to No. 1 The Parade c.1900.

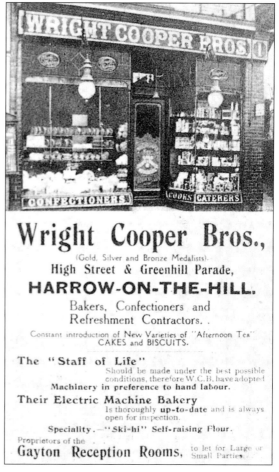

131. *Station Road before 1914. Harrow-on-the-Hill Station was then a Metropolitan and Great Central Line Station.*

1928. The premises were extended in 1935 and again in 1937 onto empty building plots in Greenhill Crescent. The old Marquis of Granby, which had been rebuilt in 1925, closed down in 1960 and the store took over the site and gradually between 1962-7 filled in all the area between Station Road and Greenhill Road.[12] The name was changed to Debenham's in December 1972

Greenhill never attracted industries as Wealdstone had, but did have two concerns, Westerdick's Joinery Works and Rothwell's Organ Factory. Westerdick's started in 1913 and did well during the First World War by building side-cars which were in demand by the army. The firm moved from Byron Road to Elmgrove Road in 1920. Frederick Rothwell's organ workshop was established in Bonnersfield Lane in 1922. He, and his son Dudley, after him, supplied and repaired organs. Examples may be found at St John's, Greenhill and at St John's, Great Stanmore. When Dudley Rothwell retired in 1964 the factory closed and was used as a library administrative centre and store from 1965-72.

The *Harrow Gazette* was established in the High Street on the Hill in 1855. As Greenhill developed, another newspaper, the *Harrow Observer*, was started near the Havelock Arms in Station Road in April 1895. Harrow thus had two newspapers until 1921, when the *Gazette* was taken over by the *Observer* which has done sterling work since keeping the community informed about events and changes and providing a forum for lively discussion. The *Observer* moved from its first offices in 1960 to a new block replacing

132. *Charles Watson's shop was at Greenhill Parade in St Ann's Road.*

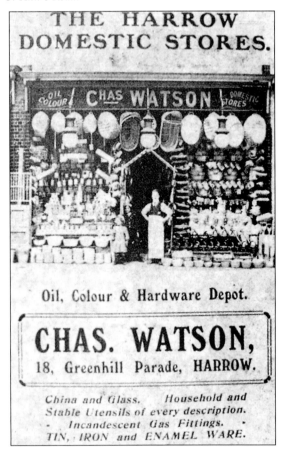

133. *Station Road with the luxurious 2000-seater Coliseum cinema on the right, which was opened in 1920 by Oswald Mosley, then the local MP. It became a theatre in 1939 under the direction of Alfred Denville. It was closed in June 1956, following his death in 1955 and was demolished in 1958.*

Ann's Place, then again in May 1984 to Greenhill Way and finally, in May 1988, came back to Station Road not far from its original office.

ST ANNE'S & ST GEORGE'S SHOPPING CENTRES[13]

After the Second World War there were various plans for the development of Harrow. The scheme which produced St Anne's (the planners added an 'e' to St Ann) shopping centre, published in 1968, stated baldly that Harrow Town Centre needed to be saved from slow strangulation and that this could only be done by a single comprehensive scheme of development. Greenhill had become Harrow Town in the eyes of councillors and planners who often have little sense of history. The ancient town on top of the hill had long ceased to be the centre of trade and commerce.

The scheme which aimed to provide first-class shops was intended to be completed by 1980. It involved demolishing practically everything between College and St Ann's Road, sparing only the purpose built shops around the Station Road and St Ann's Road frontages and the Royal Oak in St Ann's Road (now the Rat and Parrot).

There was an inquiry opened in April 1970 and there were objections. The Friends of the Earth, mixing their metaphors, said that 'central Harrow in ten years time would be a concrete jungle, just a cardboard shopping centre'.

St Anne's Centre opened in 1987. Work then began on the area to the west and St George's shopping centre, which houses the Warner Village Cinema Complex was ready in 1996.

[1] Harrow Central Reference Library.

[2] Wilkins, Harry: *Greenhill from village to Harrow Town Centre* London Borough of Harrow (1981).

[3] Harrow Central Reference Library: Farm File.

[4] Harrow Central Reference Library: Smith, Thomas: *Handbook for the use of visitors to Harrow on the Hill*, 1850

[5] Wilkins, Harry: *op. cit.*

[6] Harrow Central Reference Library: Farm File

[7] Harrow Central Reference Library: Sales Details.

[8] Wilkins, Harry: *op. cit.*

[9] *Victoria County History, Middlesex*, Vol IV, p261.

[10] Information from N. Kember.

[11] Wilkins, Harry: *op. cit.*

[12] Harrow Central Reference Library: Central Harrow Shops File.

[13] Harrow Central Reference Library: Harrow Town Centre Plans.

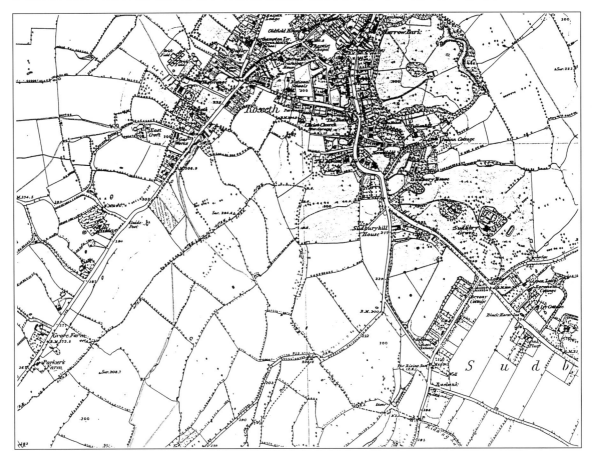

134. Roxeth on the six-inch Ordnance Survey Map 1868.

Roxeth becomes South Harrow

PATTERN OF DEVELOPMENT

The long hamlet of Roxeth straggled along its green from the junction of Lowlands and Pinner Road to the boundary of Northolt at Petts Hill. There was no obvious centre until a number of cottages were built at the bottom end of Middle Road and Roxeth Hill between the time of the enclosure of 1817 and the surveying of the 1868 Ordnance Survey map. This area became known as Roxeth Corner. The Timber Truck, the Half Moon and the White Horse public houses and several shops were situated there. Building in Victorian times was on the slope of Harrow Hill and along the roadside pieces of the former green. The next phase of development began with the opening of South Harrow Station in 1903 on farmland south-west of the railway line. After the coming of the Piccadilly Line with through trains to central London in 1933, the rest of the farmland and the former open fields of Roxeth were covered with houses and there has been much redevelopment of Northolt Road north east of the station since the 1960s.

135. Roxeth Corner, Northolt Road c.1905.

136. South Harrow Station c.1935.

137.   Roxeth Grange, an engraving by Thomas Barber, 1879. The house was later known as Grange Farm.

ROXETH'S FARMS

All but one of the ten farmhouses that appear on the 1864 OS six-inch map disappeared during the twentieth century. The moated site and great barn of the old manor was at Grange Farm almost opposite Roxeth Corner. The 1547 Terrier[1] mentions the manor farm at Roxeth 'whereupon is builded no mansion or house but a barn'. It was leased by the Archbishop of Canterbury to John Webbe in 1540, at £6 per annum and 33s 2d quit rent.[2] The great barn was not repaired after being hit by a flying bomb during the war and was demolished in 1948. However there was a house on the site at the time of the enclosures. Richard Chapman, farmer and builder, acquired it by marriage from the Greenhills in the mid-nineteenth century, farming 100 acres at the time of the 1851 census. He probably altered or rebuilt the house. Hall's Dairy Farm moved to Grange Farm from Eastcroft Farm in 1909. The farmhouse was demolished and sold for building in 1962 and the Grange Estate, built with a special glass fibre material known as resiform, said to be more enduring than bricks and mortar, replaced the old manor moat, farm and barn in 1969.

There were three farms at the southern end of Roxeth, Parker's, Grove and Barnett's Farms.

Parker's Farm at Stroud Gate took its name from James Parker, farmer there in 1850.[3] Sales details of 1879 when J.H. Anthony Esq was selling the farmhouse, a labourer's cottage and 86 acres of land, note that it was then on lease to Mr Daniel Hawkins 'the well-known horse-dealer' at an 'inadequate rent' of £300 per annum.[4] The farm, being a head tenement, still owed a heriot of 10s to the lord of the manor. The land was described as 'suitable for building development' although in fact building did not start on the farm until 1909 and the farmhouse disappeared between the two world wars.

Grove Farm[5] was on the opposite side of Northolt Road and may have been the tenement called Webbs in the sixteenth century. The name was changed to The Grove in 1721 by Samuel Sandford who had purchased it in 1717. The Hollis family were in possession by 1746 until the time of the enclosure, but it probably passed into the hands of J.H. Anthony soon afterwards. In 1825 William Baker moved in as tenant with his new wife. He was embarking upon both marriage and a career in farming at the age of 19. The couple were blessed with ten children,

138. Grove Farm c.1912 at the time that it became The Paddocks.

one of whom, Robert, ran the farm after his father's death in 1871. Robert's wife, Mary, died at the farm in tragic circumstances on 7 February 1887. While Robert was out with his son at the Lyceum Theatre seeing Henry Irving in *Faust*, the house caught fire and upon his return at 1.15 am he was able to get no further than the parlour because of smoke and flames. He could not find his wife and wondered whether she had gone to a neighbour's to seek help. By the time the fire brigade arrived at 2.00 am the house was little more than a shell and eight of the fire-fighters were injured when the front wall fell while they were trying to extinguish the flames. Mary Baker's remains were discovered in the kitchen next morning and carried to Barnett's Farm nearby. It was later suggested that the fire was caused by Mrs Baker upsetting an oil lamp.

A new house was built on the site of the old, which one assumes from its age must have been timber framed. Grove and Parker's Farms were being run together as a dairying concern in the late 1890s and had become Grove Farm Dairies by 1905. The Hawkins family were involved with the running of the dairy. It changed hands

several times; William Henry Anthony was the owner in 1902 and Clarke & Co. by 1910. Alfred Benjamin Champniss about 1913 created a sports and pleasure ground on part of the farm and called it The Paddocks. He was a local councillor and after his death in 1929, 21 acres were conveyed to Harrow UDC and laid out as a public park. Following the naming of Alexandra Av-

139. This charming building, seen here in 1888, was Barnett's Farm. It was allowed to become derelict. Sainsbury's supermarket was built on the site in 1969.

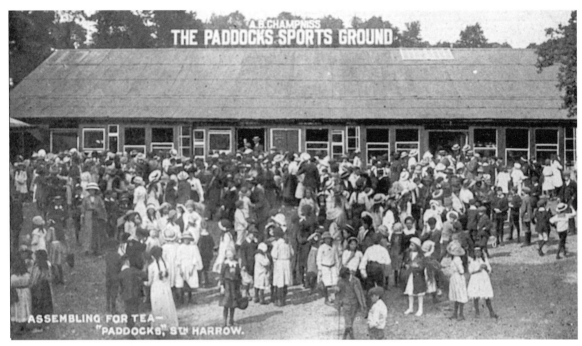

140. Happy children arriving at Mr Champniss's Sports Ground shortly before the First World War.

enue in 1930, it became Alexandra Park in 1933.

Barnett's Farm (which was sometimes called Roxeth Farm, but should not be confused with the other Roxeth Farm on Bessborough Road) near Corbins Lane, took its name from the Barnett family who farmed there from the mid-1860s until 1925. It appears to have been another sixteenth-century building with rambling additions, but it became derelict after the Second World War. Sainsbury's opened a supermarket on the site in 1969.

A little further along the road, set back was St Hilda's a seventeenth-century house which with its land was occupied by Naylor's Nurseries in the 1890s, but must have been a farmhouse at an earlier date. After Len Naylor went to Australia after the First World War, part of the house was used as an 'open house' for young people from the various churches.[6] St Hilda's Hall alongside a former stable and hayloft in the yard behind had a fine dance floor and was opened as a dance hall by Walter Farr of Farr's School of Dancing in 1925. The Baptist church has been on the site since 1935 and St Hilda's Hall is used as the church hall.

Roxborough, Honeybun and Roxeth (known as Woodbridges) Farms were at the northern end

of Roxeth in Bessborough Road.

The Atkins family had lived at Honeybun's or Honeybone's Farm in Bessborough Road since 1803, turning their hands to all kinds of trades, timber merchants, ladder and barrow-making and selling coal. Harrow UDC built their first council houses on the site in 1920. The *Harrow Observer* reported that three houses were up and that the farmhouse was being demolished in February that year. An Atkins was the first licensee of the Timber Truck (now Timber Car-

141. Roxborough Farm.

142. *St Hilda's, Northolt Road, where the Naylor family lived and had a nursery garden.*

143. *Roxeth (Woodbridges) Farm, Bessborough Road. This is the only farmhouse left standing in Roxeth. It is now a private house.*

riage) which opened in the 1830s and took its name from the trucks arriving at Atkins yard. The present pub was built in 1936.

Two Greenhills, Joseph and William were farming at Roxborough Farm in the middle of the century.

Out of all the farms, Roxeth Farm[7] is the sole survivor, though now a private residence. It very nearly suffered the same fate as the others, having been declared unfit for human habitation in 1955. The Medical Officer of Health confirmed that necessary repairs would be unreasonably costly. Although a listed building, the then owners, Harrow School, could not bear the cost and were willing to sell it to a firm of builders. After a struggle, because the council was unwilling to grant a demolition order, and remonstrations from Tom Bartlett, Secretary of the Friends of Roxeth, an architect restored the house and converted it into two flats to be occupied by Lane and Bridge, chartered accountants. The Lane family in fact occupied it as a single house.

Tithe Farm was a new farm built after the enclosure of 1817 on a rectorial tithe allotment. The Tithe Farm Public House at the corner of Alexandra Avenue and Eastcote Lane was built on the site of the barn in 1935. The farmhouse survived until after the Second World War, but Rowe Walk now marks the spot where it once stood.

GENTRY

Three of the people who were classified as gentry in Smith's *Handbook for visitors to Harrow-on-the-Hill* in 1850, lived in Roxeth Villas. Two were at Roxeth Cottage, two at Dudley Cottage (the curate of St Mary's and a female relative) and one at Roxeth House. All these buildings have disappeared.

144. *The Territorial HQ in Northolt Road where the Church Lads' Brigade first met in 1894.*

145. *Roxeth Gas Works c.1911. The gas works was a major employer in Roxeth.*

GAS[8]

As Roxeth developed in Victorian times, those who were not employed on the farms or in shops, either worked for Harrow School (the laundry was built in Alma Road in 1887) or at the Gas Works. John Chapman opened the gasworks in 1855 at the instigation of Dr Vaughan, headmaster of Harrow School, to provide domestic gas and street lighting. The Harrow Gas, Light and Coke Co Ltd was formed in 1872 and became the Harrow District Gas Company the following year. After joining with the Great Stanmore Company in 1894 and being taken over by Brentford Gas Company in 1924 it became part of North Thames Gas Board in 1949.

The gasometer which was such a landmark was erected in 1931 by Cutler's, the builders. It caused controversy at the time as it intruded on the view from Harrow Hill made famous by Byron. On a notorious occasion it was confused with a similar one at Southall by the pilot of a large 'plane heading for Heathrow, causing him to land at Northolt Aerodrome by mistake. It was impossible for so heavy a plane to take off from the short runway there without having all the seating removed! A large white arrow and the letters 'NO' were painted on the side of the gasholder to prevent future mistakes. It was demolished in 1986. Gas was not produced at Roxeth after 1954 when it became the Harrow Holder Station and Depot. A Waitrose supermarket opened on the site in 1996 and gasworkers' cottages had been replaced by Bovis House in 1964-5. John Chapman is commemorated in the east window at Christ Church.

The Three Horseshoes near the gas works was Roxeth's oldest hostelry having been licensed since 1751. It was a handy port of call for the thirsty gas workers who were not supposed to drink alcohol while on duty. They could climb over a side wall and slip into the Horseshoes unnoticed by anyone in authority.

146. The view from the terrace below the churchyard was slightly spoiled by the gasometer at Roxeth gasworks, built in 1931 and demolished in 1986.

HOSPITALS[9]

The Cottage Hospital was opened at Vine Cottages on Roxeth Hill in 1866. It provided nine beds and was under the care of a board of trustees which included Dr Whitfield Hewlett as medical director. He was the son of Dr Thomas Hewlett, the School Surgeon who lived next to the King's Head in Harrow High Street. There was one paid nurse and voluntary helpers were organised by Miss Constance Hewlett, Dr Thomas Hewlett's daughter. The cottages however, had bad drains and were not really suitable for the purpose, so a local man, Charles Leaf, provided land in Lower Road and a new 11-bed

147. The Three Horseshoes, the inn where gas workers slaked their thirst.

148. Harrow Hospital opened in Vine Cottages in 1866, moved to Lower Road in 1872 and finally to this decorative building designed by Arnold Mitchell, in 1907.

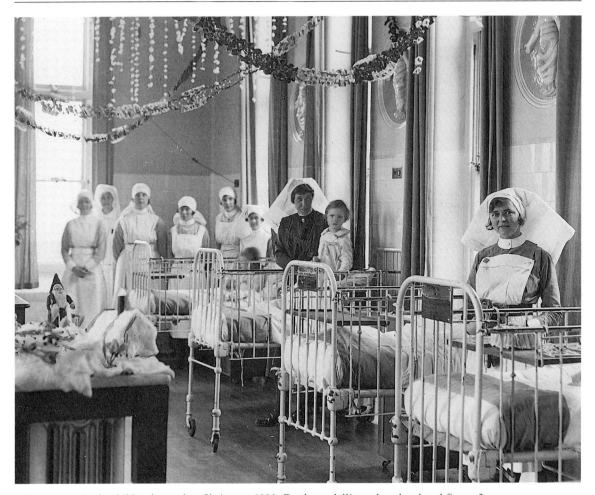

149. A scene in the children's ward at Christmas 1929. Do the medallions show bandaged figures?

hospital was opened in 1872. It included an operating-room and a dispensary. There was a sliding scale of charges ranging from 9d a day for labourers to 1s 3d a day for domestic servants in service. Small shopkeepers, being considered less well off were charged only a shilling. The present hospital was built on Roxeth Hill 1905-7 to the designs of Arnold Mitchell and an extension was built in 1931 in memory of J.N. Stuart who had been president from 1921-28. The old vicarage of Christ Church was put into use as a nurses' hostel in 1938. The hospital became a Geriatric Unit in 1974, the first phase of Northwick Park Hospital having just been completed, and closed in 1998. The building has since been listed.

The hospital depended upon the goodwill of the public for financial support. It was feared that this would be lost in July 1898 when ugly rumours began to circulate that a nurse had denied succour to two badly burnt vagrants. The couple had been hurt in a fire in a barn at Grove Farm, where they were lodging along with other itinerant hay-makers. They had been conveyed in a cart to Hendon Union Infirmary, six or seven miles away, and their groans had distressed householders along the route. The man had died next day. In fact the nurse at the hospital was not to blame as the police surgeon had sent the injured pair direct to Hendon. When criticism was expressed at a Harrow District Council meeting, he said that they had had 'a very comfortable cart to go in' and a Mr Job pointed out that the cottage hospital was not a public institution. The Revd Mr Silvester refuted this as it was run on public subscriptions. There was

150. *Northolt Road, Roxeth.*

general agreement that it would have been more merciful to detain the cases at Harrow.

An isolation hospital, opened in 1894 in Rayners Lane and known colloquially as the Fever Hospital, became a unit for the elderly and chronic sick in 1948 and was renamed Roxbourne Hospital. It closed in 1993 and was subsequently demolished.

151. *Christ Church was built in Roxeth Hill in 1862 to the designs of Sir George Gilbert Scott.*

ROXETH CHURCHES

Christ Church, in Roxeth Hill, was designed by Sir George Gilbert Scott and opened in 1862, a year after his Vaughan Library and seven years after his chapel had been built for the school. It is flint faced and nestles decoratively into the hillside. A north aisle was added *c.*1870 and there is a modern extension by K.C. White & Partners of 1979, which is attached to the main church at the western end. The vicarage of 1884-6 which became a nurses' home, is by George & Peto. There is a modern vicarage in the churchyard.

The Revd John Floyd Andrewes, vicar from 1877-1907, beautified the church with Italian marble and mosaics, and also raised money for a parish hall in Northolt Road. It was designed by Arnold Mitchell and opened in 1898. Previously the barn at Grange Farm had been used for social activities. A soup kitchen was run by the church in hard winters, providing a half-quartern loaf and a quart of soup for one penny. A company of the Church Lads' Brigade was opened at Christ Church by the curate, Mr Bull, in 1894 and their field is at the bottom of Ashbourne Avenue.

*152. The Revd John Floyd Andrewes, vicar 1877-1907
who beautified the church.*

St Paul's in Corbins Lane started as a mission from Christ Church in 1928. The first church of wood and asbestos, but none-the-less attractive, was replaced in 1937 by the present structure of grey brick designed by N.F. Cachemaille-Day.

South Harrow Baptist Mission started in 1908 in a tin chapel opposite Valentine Road. It became separate from Harrow Baptists in 1926 and a church was opened on the corner of Scarsdale Road in 1928. Within a few years the valuable site was sold for shop development and the Baptists moved to St Hilda's Hall in September 1935 and opened the present church in December of that year

John Wesley is said to have preached at the Great Barn at Grange Farm. Certainly his followers were sufficiently numerous to have a Sunday School at Mr Powell's shop in West Street by 1810 and to open a chapel for about 150 people on Roxeth Hill shortly afterwards. A grander building was erected in Lower Road about 1855 which sufficed until 1905, when a new chapel, in Gothic style, and large enough for 650 people was erected in Bessborough Road. The former meeting place, plain and dignified in appearance, served as a furniture repository and a school before becoming the Welsh Chapel.

*153. The hall and Sunday Schools of Christ Church
built in 1898.*

Following the development of the suburb of South Harrow, another Methodist church was built at the corner of Walton and Carlyon Avenues in 1937 and rebuilt in 1957.

The church of St Gabriel at the southern end of Northolt Road was built in 1933 during the expansion of the new suburb of South Harrow.

The Middlesex New Synagogue, a Reform, was opened in 1959 and took over a Victorian building in Bessborough Road in 1963. A new synagogue on the site was dedicated in 1977.

ROXETH SCHOOLS

The vicar of Harrow, the Revd Mr Cunningham, founded a school in 1812, which became a National School four years later. Lord Shaftesbury provided the National School buildings which still stand on Roxeth Hill in 1850 in memory of his son, Anthony Francis Henry Ashley, who had died at the age of 16 whilst at Harrow School. An infants' block was added at right angles in 1854. There were teachers' houses alongside. All were designed by E.H. Habershon in the gothic style.[10] The main school has a bell turret. The school had to be extended in 1898 when there were more than 600 pupils. The infants went to a new school at Welldon Park opened in 1912. A new school was erected higher up the hill in 1973.

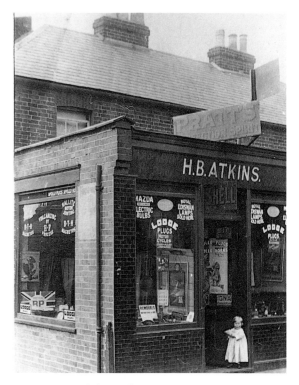

155. 174 Northolt Road c.1922.

154. The Church Lads' Brigade church in Brigade Close, built after 1909 and first used as a meeting hall. The group is now called the Roxeth & Harrow Church Lads' and Church Girls' Brigade.

156. Grange Road, South Harrow, a picture from the Harrow Observer of 31 July 1970. From left to right the residents are Mrs Minty, Mr and Mrs Harry Leaper, Mrs Jean Geed, Mrs Ellen Markham and Mrs Grace Oliver. The terrace was demolished in 1972.

Several other schools were provided for the expanding suburb. Roxeth Manor Primary in 1933 and Grange in 1949 along with Welldon Park, supplied education for junior age children. Senior schools were Roxeth Manor Secondary 1933 and Lascelles Secondary Modern 1949. They are now known as Rooks Heath and Whitmore respectively.

MODERN DEVELOPMENT

South Harrow Station opened in South Hill Avenue in 1903 for the Metropolitan District Railway. Trains ran to Hanger Lane Junction where a connection could be caught to Town. Otherwise anyone working in London must walk over the hill to the Metropolitan Line Station. The first new roads were laid out on the south side of the station, on a long field known as the Park where the Drag Hunt had formerly met and

from whose surface balloon ascents had taken place. Laid out as the Welldon Park Estate, development began after 140 building plots were auctioned by the Town and Country Land Company in 1899. Parkfield, Whitby (originally St Hilda's), Eastcote, Scarsdale, Welldon Park (later Kingsley) Roads were named in 1899 and 1900.

When the Piccadilly Line started using the same track from 1933 trains ran straight through to central London, making daily travel much simpler and giving a further impetus to building development. Most of the former farmland was covered by housing before 1939. The present station was built on the main road, designed by Stanley A. Heaps with Charles Holden in 1935 and gave rise to modern shop development alongside. The District Line went out of operation in this area after the Second World War. The area became generally known as South Harrow and the old name of Roxeth was lost.

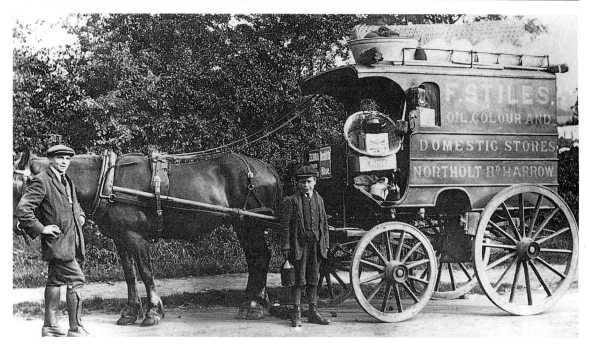

157. *A scene in Northolt Road c.1910, before modern developments turned Roxeth into South Harrow.*

Some small industrial concerns opened under the railway viaduct and a razor blade factory operated in Eastcote Lane from before the First World War. It became in turn a printer's in the late 1920s, then Eastcote Engineering and Delta Metals which closed down in 1981. There are now old people's flats on the site.

The building of office blocks and flats and superstores has completely changed the face of Roxeth since the 1960s, sweeping away the artisans' cottages and small shops as well as the farmhouses. Only Harrow School Cricket Field along the edge of Lower and Bessborough Roads retains some glimmer of the rural past.

SOURCES

Bartlett, T.L: *The Story of Roxeth,* Foy Publications (1948).

Cooper, Elizabeth: *Harrow Walkabout,* Pinner and Hatch End WEA (1973).

Harrow before your time, Pinner and Hatch End WEA Local History Group (1972).

Victoria County History of Middlesex, Vol IV, Oxford University Press (1971).

[1] LMA: Acc 1052.

[2] *Ibid.*

[3] Harrow Central Reference Library: Smith, Thomas: *Handbook for use of visitors to Harrow-on-the-Hill* (1850).

[4] LMA: Acc 507/34.

[5] Harrow Central Reference Library: Roxeth Local History Society *Newsletter*, No 8, October 1987.

[6] Bartlett, T.L. *The Story of Roxeth,* Foy Publications (1948).

[7] Harrow Central Reference Library: Farms File.

[8] *Harrow Before Your Time:* Pinner and Hatch End Local History Group (1972).

[9] *Ibid.*

[10] Cherry & Pevsner: *The Buildings of England London 3 North West* (1991).

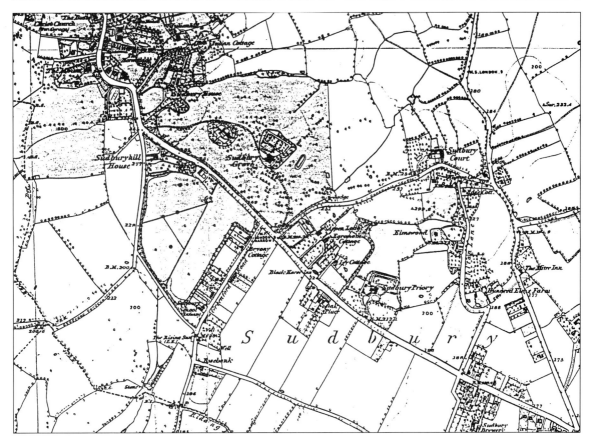

158. Sudbury on the six-inch Ordnance Survey Map 1868.

Sudbury

Sudbury, like Roxeth was a long hamlet, stretching down Sudbury Hill and along the Harrow Road, but had three recognisable settlements: around Sudbury Court (the Rectory Manor house); on the slope of Sudbury Hill to the north west; and around the Swan, a coaching inn on the Harrow Road to the south east. Sudbury Station, which opened in 1844, became Wembley Central and Sudbury itself was included in Wembley Urban District in 1895, so the two areas merge into each other.

GENTLEMEN'S HOUSES

Although in 1850[1] Sudbury had almost the same number of farmers and traders as Roxeth, far more gentlemen had made their homes there, employing a number of domestic servants (21 male and 53 female in the 1851 census) and

encouraging tradesmen and shopkeepers. There was even a 'teacher of the Piano Forte',[2] H. Tillyard at Woodside Cottage.

The late eighteenth and early nineteenth century was a period when it was fashionable for professional men and superior merchants to seek a rural retreat near London in rustic 'cottages', far removed in size, fittings and furniture from those inhabited by agricultural labourers. There were at least six such cottages in Sudbury in 1850, along with Sudbury Lodge, Sudbury Grove, Sudbury Hill House, Sudbury House, and Sudbury Priory. Did the mail ever get mixed up? Four of these genteel households were headed by women in 1850: the Misses Copland at Sudbury Lodge, the Misses Lang and Mrs Wise at Sudbury Hill House, Miss Jane Price at Woodlands Cottage and Mrs Trenchard at Aspen Lodge. The large houses seemed to change

159. *Looking down Sudbury Hill before the First World War. The house on the right is The Orchard, which Arnold Mitchell built for himself in an Arts and Crafts style in 1900.*

hands fairly frequently. Cluny MacPherson, a Highland Chief, occupied The Mount, at the top of Sudbury Hill.

The Clementine Churchill Hospital, opened in 1981 on the site of Sudbury Grove. Excavations by Wembley History Society in 1971 found pottery and domestic items dating from the thirteenth, sixteenth and seventeenth century and remains of the early nineteenth century building.[3] An earlier house had been occupied by such people as Lord Grandeson, the Duchess of Marlborough and Richard Page in the eight-

eenth century. It was purchased from Lord Northwick by Charles Hamilton Esq before 1826, who probably built the new house. Henry Young, a solicitor who had taken over the Page estates was the owner by 1850 until his death in 1869 after which Alfred Blyth acquired it.

The neighbouring properties Aspen Lodge, Egremont Cottage and Sudbury Priory on the south-east side of Sudbury Court Road, can all be seen on the enclosure map of 1817. The widowed Mrs Trenchard at Aspen Lodge had four daughters; William Clayton, a barrister was at Egremont Cottage in 1850 and William Webster, an attorney at Sudbury Priory. Mr Webster had erected a new residence in 1828 on the site of one owned by Lady Sarah Fane at the time of the enclosure.[4] All three houses had gone by the end of the 1950s. The area between Priory Gardens and Priory Hill marks the site of the house called Sudbury Priory. Sudbury Hill Close and Sudbury Croft have replaced the cottages.

Sudbury House, quite near the top of the hill, predated the enclosures and was occupied by Richard Orford Holte in 1850. It was demolished and replaced by a block of flats called Herga Court in 1936.

Julian Hill appears on Greenwood's map of 1819. Thomas Trollope, the unbalanced and unsuccessful lawyer and father of Anthony Trollope the novelist, was encouraged by his wife to try his hand at farming. He leased Ilotts

160. *Sudbury House was replaced by Herga Court in 1935.*

161. *Arnold Mitchell gave Orley Farm School several attractive features, including the crow-stepped gables and circular windows. It was built in 1900-1.*

Farm on the edge of Sudbury common from Lord Northwick about 1815 and built Julian Hill nearby, calling it after a property in Hertfordshire from which he had expectations. He let the new house and lived with his family in Ilotts farmhouse, which became the model for Anthony Trollope's 'Orley Farm'. The expected inheritance failed to materialise and Mr Trollope was caught up in the agricultural depression which affected all the local farmers in the 1820s. He took another farm in Harrow Weald (not identified) which his son described in his memoirs as 'one of those farmhouses which seem always to be in danger of falling down' and after a few years returned to Ilotts, which he is reputed to have spent £3000 on rebuilding. In 1834 he fled to Belgium to escape his creditors. Julian Hill was let to the vicar of Harrow, the Revd J.W. Cunningham. It survives divided into three houses. The Ilotts farm house became Orley Farm School, but Arnold Mitchell designed a new building for the school in South Hill Avenue in 1900-1. The farm house was demolished soon afterwards.

162. *Sudbury Hill House, which had housed the Bowden House Psychiatric Clinic, became Harrow School Sanatorium in 1929.*

COPLANDS & BARHAMS

Crabs House was built after the Messeder map of 1759 was drawn, but before the end of the eighteenth century. The grounds are now Barham Park. John Copland (1760-1843) bought it from John Crab in 1801 and his daughters, Frances and Anne built a new house alongside about 1850, called Sudbury Lodge. Anne, who died in 1872, left the estate to General Robert FitzGerald Crawford, on condition that he took the name Copland.

The Misses Copland were public benefactors, providing land for a church, building a vicarage, founding a Church of England School and a hospital. St John the Evangelist, designed by Sir George Gilbert Scott, was built in 1846 and had a north aisle, also by Scott, added in 1859. It has a fancy-tiled roof, flint walls and a bell-turret. A south aisle designed by H.R. Breakspear, a former churchwarden, was added in 1900 and a baptistry and choir vestry in 1935.[5] The school functioned until 1879 when a better school had been built at Alperton, after which it was used as a Sunday School and the school house was made into a verger's cottage. The school was demolished in 1972 following a fire the previous year.

Miss Frances Copland provided a Workmen's Hall in 1869 to house the Wembley Institute which had been founded in 1864 to enable the members to develop habits of temperance and industry. The Institute moved in 1929 and Wembley post office was built on the site in 1930. Anne Copland started the Copland Sudbury Village Hospital in 1871 for the sick poor of Wembley and neighbourhood on land next to the institute. Unfortunately the endowment, an

164. George Titus Barham built Sudbury Lodge alongside Crabs House. The new house became Barham Mansion.

investment in LNWR, was insufficient to keep the hospital going beyond 1883. The money was used to fund a hospital savings scheme, which enabled poor subscribers to get medical treatment in other hospitals and at the dispensary which continued in the hospital building for a time, before becoming a private house called Elmwood. The builder J.W. Comben (Comben & Wakeling) demolished it in 1928 to make way for the Majestic Cinema.

After General Copland-Crawford's death in 1895, Sir George Barham (1836-1913) of Express Dairy fame bought the estate and lived in Crabs House which was renamed Old Court, while his son George Titus Barham had Sudbury Lodge which became Barham Mansion. George Titus Barham was about to become Mayor of Wembley

163. Crabs House, later called Old Court, Sudbury (part of which is now the public library).

165. St John the Evangelist church, Sudbury, was built in 1846 and designed by Sir George Gilbert Scott.

in July 1937 when the borough received its charter, but sadly died just before taking office. He left the estate for the use of the people of Wembley. The house was demolished in 1956, but other buildings, including a portion of Crabs House, accommodate Barham Park Library, reception rooms and an old people's home.[6]

SIR WILLIAM HENRY PERKIN 1836-1907

W.H. Perkin was born in Shadwell, the son of a builder and developed an early interest in chemistry. He was a pupil of Hofmann at the Royal College of Chemistry. When only 18 he discovered a method of making a permanent purple dye, during an experiment to try to produce synthetic quinine. With his father and an older brother, Thomas, he opened a factory at Greenford in 1857, near the canal, to produce the aniline dye commercially and continued with his chemical experimentation. He developed a cheaper method of manufacturing artificial alizarin which helped the coal tar industry, and published a description of 'Perkin Synthesis' of unsaturated organic acids in 1867.

When he married his cousin in 1859, he came to live in the Harrow Road in Sudbury and shortly afterwards in Seymour Villa. His wife died of consumption after only two years, leaving him with two sons and he married again in 1866 and had several more children. He built The Chestnuts beside Seymour Villa and used the old house

167. The Chestnuts was the home which William Perkin built for his family in Harrow Road.

as a laboratory. After selling the Greenford factory in 1874 because of German competition, he devoted himself to experimental chemistry, investigating the constitution of chemical molecules. He became a Fellow of the Royal Society in 1866 and was president of the Chemical Society 1883-5 and of the Society of Chemical Industry 1884-5.[7]

Around Sudbury and Roxeth, however, he was known more for his good works and musical ability than his scientific achievements. He provided a 'New Hall' to replace the Coplands' Workmen's Club and made it into a meeting place for religious groups and other activities in 1878, and enthusiastically supported Sunday Schools, teaching the children; he also played his trombone and scrambled for aniseed balls at treats. The New Hall was made over to the Wesleyan Methodist Trust by his widow. He was knighted in 1906 on the fiftieth anniversary of his discovery.

At the time of his death he was regarded as the founder of the modern Chemical Industry. It was said that he was 'the first man to call into existence a completely new and mighty industry, founded on pure science'.[8] He was buried at Christ Church, Roxeth in 1907 and Tom Bartlett, who attended the funeral, remarked on the mountain of flowers and tributes then paid to his genius by German science and German industry.[9]

166. Sir William Perkin.

168.   Cottages at rear of New Hall, Sudbury, used as a Sunday School. c.1895. The whole site was made over to the Methodists in 1913 and the present church was built in 1933.

FARMING

The only working farm left in Sudbury is Harrow School Farm in Watford Road. Sudbury Court Farm, near the manor house of the Archbishop of Canterbury, was tenanted by the Hill family for the first half of the nineteenth century, then by Henry Green and from 1900 by William Perrin who was also running Lower Sudbury Court Farm (Harrow School Farm), Sudbury Farm in Watford Road near East Lane and Lyon's Farm at Preston in Harrow, as well as farms in Buckinghamshire. He was succeeded at Sudbury Court Farm by his sons, Kenneth and Edward who sold it for development in 1956. Kenelm Close is now on the site.

Two buildings at Hundred Elms Farm survive among modern housing off Elms Lane. One is the farmhouse of the 1840s and the other a reputedly sixteenth-century building of red-brick across the court yard. It has been suggested that this might have been the forerunner of Sudbury Place which is mentioned in seventeenth-century documents. The Greenhills farmed Hundred Elms for most of the nineteenth century.

Vale Farm on the edge of the common south of the Mitre was owned by the Lakes in the eighteenth century. Samuel Palmer of Huntley & Palmer's biscuits lived there from 1874-98. It was rebuilt at the end of the nineteenth century and became well-known for its dairy. It is now Vale Farm Sports Centre and the farmhouse is used by the parks department.

169. Vale Farm Dairy Milk Float.

170. Hundred Elms Farmyard contained an old brick building apparently of the Tudor period, seen on the left. Both buildings survive.

THE BREWERY AND PUBLIC HOUSES

Sudbury and Harrow Brewery still stands in Harrow Road, but no beer has been brewed since the First World War. It is now used by a building contractor. It was open by 1859 and had several owners until being taken over by Dewar Watson of Dundee and Frederick Speedy about 1870. It traded as Watson Bros Ltd from the late 1870s until about 1916. Dewar Watson lived at Northwick House until 1905. The Jolly Gardeners, dating from about 1870, was the tied beer house. It disappeared between the wars.

The Mitre and the Swan were both licensed in the eighteenth century, in 1756 and 1786 respectively and both were later owned by Clutterbuck's, the Stanmore brewers. The Mitre was rebuilt in 1933, but the Swan remains in its old building. The Black Horse was licensed to Sarah Howard in 1751 and also owned by Clutterbuck's by the time of the enclosure. Horse-drawn omnibus services were run from here to Sudbury Station in the 1860s and by Mr Groom, a later licensee, into the twentieth century.

MOUNT PARK ESTATE

The Mount is an imposing early nineteenth-century house on Sudbury Hill with an estate of 155 acres spreading across to Northolt Road. The grounds contained a round tower or folly, known as Prior Bolton's Ark (*see* p30), which had Tudor foundations. The house belonged to Samuel Hoare at the time of the Harrow enclosure and the house appears on the accompanying map of 1817. The estate was put up for sale by auction in October 1876. Advertised as 'an excellent residence with capital stabling and convenient outbuildings, extensive pleasure grounds and gardens and a compact farm homestead'[10] it was also said to be 'admirably adapted for sub-division for building purposes'. The farm at that time was let to Mr Pring, the park to Abraham Parsons and two fields to Mrs Holt. A gothic residence called Mount Lodge had been recently erected in a corner of the park at the top of what was to become Mount Park Road.

Gradually the plots for 'first-class' residences were sold during the 1880s and large houses erected, designed by popular architects like Arnold Mitchell, who was a Harrow man, and R.A. Briggs. The author of boys' adventure stories, R.M. Ballantyne, lived at Duneaves in

171. Thornlea, Mount Park Avenue

173. Sudbury Hill Station opened in 1906 and was rebuilt to Charles Holden's design, following his much acclaimed Sudbury Town Station of 1931.

the 1880s. William Winckley bought a section of the park at the first sale and divided it into 21 plots. Wendela, owned by S.H. Darwen esq, had been built on one of them by 1898. Wendela Court is now on the site. The Mount itself was purchased by nuns in 1878 and St Dominic's Convent School was established there. The chapel of 1921 and school buildings of 1928, 1937 and 1978-80 survive, but Prior Bolton's Ark was considered to be unsafe and was demolished in 1968. The convent and the school became St Dominic's Sixth Form College in 1979. The Mount

172. The Mount became St Dominic's convent in 1878. A hundred years later the interior was refashioned behind the facade and became offices, known as Bydell House. In 1998 the offices were converted into flats and the old name has been restored.

was sold and converted into offices in 1978, being named Bydell House. It has recently returned to domestic use, now being private flats. The old name has been restored.

MODERN DEVELOPMENT
The opening of Sudbury Town Station in 1903 and Sudbury Hill Station in 1906 provided for some modern shops and the usual suburban development swallowed up the Sudbury farm-land in the late 1920s and 1930s.

SOURCES
Egan, H: *Sudbury, Middlesex, a short history and guide,* British Publishing Company Ltd (1965).
Ed. Hewlett, Geoffrey: *A History of Wembley,* Brent Library Service (1979).
Ed. Pugh, R. B: *Victoria County History of Middlesex* Vol IV (1971).

[1] Smith, Thomas: *Handbook for visitors to Harrow-on-the Hill* (1850)
[2] *Ibid.*
[3] Ed. Hewlett, Geoffrey: *A History of Wembley* (1979).
[4] Harrow Central Reference Library: House Files.
[5] Cherry B. & Pevsner N: *Buildings of England: London 3: North-West,* Penguin Books (1991).
[6] Harrow Central Reference Library: House Files.
[7] *Dictionary of National Biography.*
[8] Crowther, J.G. *British Scientists of the Nineteenth Century,* Pelican (1941).
[9] Bartlett, T.L: *The Story of Roxeth,* Foy Publications Ltd (1948).
[10] Harrow Central Reference Library: Auction Catalogue of Mount Park Estate 1876.

174. Harrow-on-the-Hill High Street c. 1900.

The Town on the Hill

And so we return to the top of the hill where the story began. Unlike the hamlets of the old parish, Harrow Town was relatively unaffected by the coming of the railways and general suburban expansion. The genteel developments in Harrow Park, Roxborough Park, Peterborough Road and Grove Hill in the 1880s reflect the influence of the school, providing suitable houses for both masters and parents, as much as that of the station in Lowlands Road. The mid-Victorian terraces off West Street were sensible choices for those who provided services for the school as it expanded. The large green spaces on the south-west side of the hill and the cricket grounds on the east have been preserved by the direct intervention of the school.

In Victorian times the High Street on the hill, was the shopping centre for the whole of Harrow and the main post office, the police station and the fire station, were situated there. The gas works were at the foot of the hill in Roxeth and

175. Houses like The Firs, seen here, were built in Roxborough Park after this portion of the Northwick estate was sold in 1889.

176. The Town Pump was at the junction of High Street and West Street, in front of Goshawk's photographic studio. The pump was replaced by the present polished granite fountain in 1881.

the water works were on Bessborough Road at the bottom of the cricket grounds. Piped water was provided to subscribers' houses from 1855 onwards. The hospital was close, at the top of Roxeth Hill. The non-conformists, Methodists and Baptists, all began their ministry on the hill. The *Harrow Gazette* had its offices at 52-6 High Street from 1855.

It was a self-contained community, but a day trip to town for shopping or business was possible even before the coming of the Metropolitan Railway in 1880. In the 1850s a coach left the Crown and Anchor at the foot of Church Hill each morning at 9.00 am, reaching the Gloucester Coffee House in Oxford Street at 10.10 am and the Bull Inn, Holborn at 10.30 am. The return journey started from Holborn at 4.30 pm and got back to Harrow at 6.00 pm.[1] Visitors to the hill who enjoyed walking were encouraged to travel from London to Ealing by the Great Western Railway and then make their way on foot through Perivale churchyard, Greenford and Sudbury, which would take them through 'some of the most secluded and beautiful portions of the Vale' (Perivale).[2] The King's Head with Livery and

177. The heavily tile-decorated Garlands in Peterborough Road was the work of C. F. Hayward and was built in 1863.

178. *A somewhat overloaded coach stands outside the King's Head in the 1870s.*

179. *The Methodist Chapel in Lower Road from 1855 to the beginning of the twentieth century. It is now a Welsh Chapel.*

180. *The police station in West Street opened in 1873 in front of the old station.*

181. The Square at the junction of High Street and London Road. The sign advertises the King's Head, off the picture to the right. The Bank, the cottage and a glimpse of the Fire Station can be seen. On the left of the picture is the row of late Victorian shops in gothic style built 1868-72. The building with the imposing doorway beyond the shops was the public hall of 1874.

Bait stables and horses for hire, was 'the principal hotel, conducted by Mr James Laws'. The Crown and Anchor, also with Livery and Bait stables, had been in the hands of the Bliss family 'for more than a hundred years'. Ephraim Terry and William Hartmann both kept Livery Stables and the Castle and the Crown were licensed to hire out horses.[3]

Smith's handbook lists 39 gentry living on the hill, of whom 16 are masters or assistant masters at the school and there were nearly 100 tradesmen, in 1850. They include bakers, confectioners and pastry cooks; milliners and dressmakers, straw hat and bonnet makers; tailors and boot and shoemakers; bookseller and stationer; plumbers, glaziers, carpenters and ironmongers and dealers in tea etc. The most unusual tradesman was the suitably named Edmund Goshawk, 'haircutter and bird stuffer' *(see* p79). There was no industry on the hill.

Victorian Harrow was thriving and new civic and commercial buildings were erected which matched those of the school for grandeur. The old police station in West Street was replaced in 1873 by a building designed by R.H. Cager and erected by Fassnidge, the Uxbridge builder. The London County Bank (1883) and a new Fire

182. The wall of a timber-framed house was discovered during renovations at 52-56 High Street following damage by traffic.

183. The central building was built in 1872 and the post office moved there in 1879.

184. The London County Bank of 1889 is on the left of this picture and the Fire Station of 1888 on the right. It functioned until 1963. The cottage between was demolished in 1913 to make way for the Harrow Urban District Council Offices.

Station (1888) were built beyond the King's Head. The cottage between them was demolished in 1914 to make way for Harrow Urban District Council Offices. A row of shops opposite, of highly decorative brickwork, included the first purpose-built post office

But the balance of population between the hill and Greenhill was changing. Wright Cooper and other tradesmen saw where the future lay and moved down to the north side of Harrow-on-the Hill station. Popular entertainment in the form of cinemas opened there too, and the main Post Office followed. The hill was left more or less in peace to brood over the ever-changing maelstrom below.

[1] Smith, Thomas: *Handbook for the use of visitors to Harrow-on-the-hill* (1850).

[2] *Ibid.*

[3] *Ibid.*